WORLD WAR II COMMANDERS

WORLD WAR II COMMANDERS

FROM THE ATTACK ON POLAND TO THE SURRENDER OF JAPAN

Ian Westwell

COMPENDIUM

This 2008 edition published by

COMPENDIUM

© 2008 by Compendium
Publishing Ltd. 43 Frith Street,
London W1D 4SA, United Kingdom

The Author

Ian Westwell is a military historian
and author who has written and /or
contributed to several military books
and periodicals. Among his most
recent works have been *World War
One Day By Day*, *The Encyclopedia of
World War I*, *In the Path of the Third
Reich*, and *1st Infantry Division*.

Project Manager: Ray Bonds
Designer: Cara Rogers
Color Reproduction:
Anorax Imaging Ltd

ISBN: 978-1-906347-31-4

Printed and bound in China

Contents

Additional illustrations

Page 1: Following the Blitzkrieg campaign across northern France, like tourists seeing the sights of Paris, Hitler and his staff pose for a picture with the Eiffel Tower in the background,

Pages 2-3: General Eisenhower gives men of the US 101st Airborne Division a pep talk on the eve of the Normandy invasion, June 1944.

Left: Homecoming hero General George S. Patton enjoys the adulation of the crowds in Manhattan, New York City.

Introduction

It is only in the comparatively recent past that men have been groomed for senior command by attending war colleges such as West Point in the United States and Sandhurst in England. For much of recorded history, military commanders have commanded because of their rank or station in life and not because of their training or combat experience. This is not to say that all those who have shown excellent generalship in the past have attended such institutions, and nor does it mean that all attendees of such colleges have proved outstanding leaders of men in battle.

In World War II senior commanders tended to have had a similar career path. A good number were career soldiers who had served in World War I as junior officers, including MacArthur, Montgomery, Patton, Rommel, and Zhukov to name but a handful. During the interwar era, they slowly rose through the officer ranks, often simply because of long service rather than by proving themselves on the battlefield. Most of them also undertook further studies, served in various staff positions largely at home but sometimes overseas, especially in the case of US and British officers. They also commanded bodies of men of various sizes but not on the scale of an army or army group, for example.

However, promotion in peacetime, especially in armies that had been much reduced in size since 1918, was rarely rapid. Nevertheless, most of the senior commanders who

Left: Eisenhower (left) shares a joke with Omar Bradley (gesticulating) while Patton and Hodges look on. "Ike" was tough and resolute, and although he had never seen action himself he won the support of front-line commanders, as well as Allied leaders.

Right: A controversial figure, Douglas MacArthur was immensely popular with the American public, and with those who served him, but many of his peers found him difficult to work with, and he frequently clashed with the political establishment.

Above: Churchill, Roosevelt, and Stalin—the "Big Three"—at the Yalta Conference in February 1945. Churchill enjoyed a good relationship with Roosevelt, and with the latter's successor, Harry S Truman. Although Britain and the United States gave financial and matériel support to the Soviets, the tripartite relationship was frequently strained and hardened after hostilities ceased.

went to war in 1939–1941 had more than two decades of military experience under their belts. Yet most would never have led more than a division and many less than that. But the war brought rapid promotion for those with the right qualities. Montgomery, for example, who was commanding a division in May 1940, had charge of a corps by the following July, and an army by November.

If many senior officers had essentially similar backgrounds with regard to training and experience, they had widely different characters that, for good or bad, had an impact on the style of their generalship. Some were largely cautious; some overly incautious. Some were regarded as caring for their men; some were not. Some shunned publicity and some actively sought it out. Some were team players but others were decidedly not. War also tends to separate the great commanders from the merely competent or even incompetent—and this was certainly true in World War II. A good number of commanders were sacked or worse, especially in Nazi Germany and the Soviet Union, although this was not always a matter of ability or the lack of it, but rather down to the whim of their political masters, Hitler and Stalin. Even Churchill proved willing to sack a general or two, particularly during the 1940–1941 period when Britain stood alone and needed a victory of some sorts in the Middle East as quickly as possible.

The generals eventually showed their mettle in battle as field commanders or as strategic overlords of several armies. This was more than a matter of scale: a good field general of a corps of, say, 50,000-plus men did not necessarily make a good army commander of 150,000 troops, and nor did a competent army commander always make a great leader of an even bigger army group. The key issue was often one of delegation, of a commander knowing where his responsibilities began and ended. A strategic vision like the broad-front strategy adopted by the western Allies for the liberation of northwest Europe in 1944-1945, for example, was thrashed out at the highest level, and then roles were delegated appropriately all the way down the chain of command.

The various wartime generals, even the best of them, were neither infallible nor unbeatable, and few would rank among the truly great military leaders. In truth, Germany produced a considerable number of outstanding commanders but none, perhaps with the exception of Manstein, would rank alongside the great captains of history. The Allies had Zhukov and Patton, and some might include Montgomery, but both of the latter two had their undeniable flaws. Neither of them was a team player; and both were great self-publicists. It was perhaps hardly

Below: President Roosevelt and General Patton append the Medal of Honor on Colonel (later Brigadier General) William H. Wilbur, while Army Chief of Staff General George C. Marshall looks on. Wilbur received the award "for conspicuous gallantry and intrepidity in action above and beyond the call of duty."

Left: As prime minister of the United Kingdom from 10 May 1940 Churchill endeared himself to the British public and members of the armed services with inspirational oratory, although he did manage to upset the military establishment with his "meddling" in strategic military affairs.

Right: Beneath a glowering sky, American troops wade ashore onto the Normandy beaches in the face of heavy German machine gun fire, June 6, 1944, during the greatest amphibious operation ever undertaken. Handling the logistics was a colossal undertaking, requiring phenomenal cooperation between the Allied leaders and their staffs. Backed by 11,000 aircraft, in just forty-eight hours almost 200,000 men and their equipment were carried and supported by five thousand ships and thousands of smaller craft across the English Channel to northern France.

surprising that they could barely stand being in the same room as each other.

The reality is that modern conflicts—and it was the same for World War II—are so complex that they are increasingly managed not by individuals but by groups of individuals, staffs who report to a supreme commander and who who sets their goals. The western Allies were especially lucky that their supreme commander, Eisenhower, was a team player with excellent man-management skills. Nazi Germany, in contrast, had a supreme commander in Hitler who had neither traits. During World War II, some senior commanders benefited from luck. However, it was a generally less important asset for victory than a general's planning, insight, knowledge, training, and expertise. While the very best commanders did rely on luck finding them by chance, they more likely made their own.

There were few senior statesmen in World War II who did not become directly involved in military matters at one level or another. Franklin D. Roosevelt, who left the fighting to the experts, was an exception, but Winston Churchill and, above all, Adolf Hitler and Joseph Stalin were often intervening in campaigns. Churchill and Hitler had some military experience, albeit at a junior level, while Stalin had none whatsoever, having been rejected for service in World War I on the grounds of physical unfitness. Yet this lack of or limited experience proved no barrier to them poring over war maps and telling generals what to do and how to do it. Their meddling was often not appreciated by the military establishment—to say the least—and often had unfortunate consequences for their respective causes.

Churchill's insistence on invading Italy in 1943, for example, condemned the Allies to a long, bitterly contested campaign that did little to significantly weaken Germany but did swallow up tens of thousands of troops that might have been better employed elsewhere. Stalin, the only political leader who exercised direct control of his country's armed forces throughout the war, made several disastrous decisions that cost the lives of many thousands of troops in the Red Army during the first six months or so

Left: A parade of the *Wehrmacht's* might in front of the Berlin Technical High School, 20 April 1939, in honor of Hitler's fiftieth birthday. This typified the rather sycophantic manner in which his officers approached the *Fuehrer*, who always wanted but didn't get until 1945 a "yes man" as chief of the army general staff.

Right: Adolf Hitler regarded himself as somewhat of a visionary in terms of warfare; he rather fancied himself as the supreme commander, the greatest in history. He did have considerable natural abilities as a general strategist, but was too prone to dabble in the day-to-day running of campaigns. As an embittered ex-infantryman he also harbored great contempt for his professional officers.

of 1942. Yet Stalin did learn the harsh lesson and began to listen to his generals, although he continued to remain suspicious of them.

Hitler, of all of the war leaders, meddled the most in purely military matters, even down to spending hours arguing over the smallest of details. He saw himself as something of a natural strategic visionary, an equal of Frederick the Great, and a leader who could readily dismiss the counsel of his generals. He increasingly began to believe that they were not committed to the Nazi cause, and often accused them of lacking ambition or of being overly pessimistic when they pointed out flaws in his plans and wanted to amend them. This friction first emerged on a large scale when the German push on Moscow in late 1941 was halted, and relations reached a nadir following the failed assassination attempt—the Bomb Plot during July 1944—in which many army officers were implicated. Unlike the Allied war leaders, Hitler rarely listened to advice from his commanders and increasingly chose to surround himself with sycophants.

His response to the reverse outside Moscow was to sack a number of generals and make himself supreme commander of the country's army. For the remainder of the war Hitler thus instigated and presided over a number of military blunders of a lesser or greater magnitude. He became especially notorious for forbidding withdrawal even when all military logic dictated that it was the right course of action. If things did go wrong with one of his plans, Hitler developed the habit of passing the blame on to one or more of his field commander and then sacking them.

However, being political leaders is about much more than becoming involved in military matters to a lesser or greater degree or for good or bad. Among other things, they have to become embroiled in all aspects of a nation's

Left: Mamoru Shigemitsu (minister of foreign affairs, with stick) and General Yoshijiro Umezu lead the Japanese delegation aboard the USS *Missouri* during the utterly humiliating surrender ceremonies on 2 September 1945.

war effort, from its economy and the welfare of its people to international and diplomatic issues. Great wartime leaders generally delegate responsibility and hopefully choose the right man (or woman). Churchill and Roosevelt largely chose correctly and operated cabinet-style govern-ments, while Stalin, who was a something of a paranoid workaholic, preferred to make all the decisions himself and tell subordinates to get on with the job.

Hitler generally gave his subordinates freer rein, preferring to concentrate on military affairs, technical matters, and foreign policy, although there was precious little of the latter in the war years. He was the self-styled political visionary, one who laid down the framework of the Third Reich but left others to bring his vision into being. Thus, for example, decisions on day-to-day matters relating to the home front were taken by men such as his chancellery chief, Hans Lammers, or Martin Bormann, his personal secretary.

The Allied war leaders proved superior to their rivals in one especially significant area. In one way or another they offered morale leadership to their people from begin-ning to end. They might have suffered from self-doubt, even depression in private—as both Churchill and Stalin did—but in public they displayed no such weakness even in the worst possible of times. Churchill was renowned for his resounding, morale-raising oratory and was not afraid to tour war-ravaged areas of London, while for his part Stalin gradually positioned himself as the defender of the Russian motherland and became, despite the brutality he inflicted on his own people, a much-revered figure until his crimes were revealed in the 1950s. Ultimately, their moral courage gave hope to those they ruled over or

served.

The same cannot be said for either Hitler or Mussolini. The latter's popularity plunged even in the first years of the war and, of course, he was eventually executed by his own people, his bullet-riddled corpse being put on humiliating display in Milan. Hitler ultimately viewed with contempt the German people and the state over which he ruled. Even when the Allied strategic bombing campaign was reducing Germany's cities to rubble one by one and killing thousands of people, he never visited the survivors or viewed the damage. Towards the end, in mid-March 1945, he even ordered the destruction of what little remained of Germany's cities and economic infrastructure. Albert Speer was ordered to carry out the scorched earth policy but argued in a face-to-face meeting that it would serve no practical purpose and merely inflict even more misery on ordinary Germans. Hitler's response was to tell Speer: "… It is better to destroy even that [the most basic human existence], and to destroy it ourselves. The nation has proved itself weak… Besides, those who remain after the battle are of little value; for the good have fallen."

Even Hitler's own courage failed him in the end. For all his talk of wanting a soldier's death amidst the ruins of Berlin, fighting to the last, he committed suicide in a fetid underground bunker. The most telling point is that Hitler and Mussolini died squalid deaths unloved by their people, while the demise of Churchill, Roosevelt, and even Stalin prompted huge outpourings of national grief. Such is the true measure of towering political leadership in the darkest of times.

Readers should note that, in the alphabetical descriptions of leaders in the following pages, the terms "senior position" and "final rank" refer to those held exclusively during World War II and not subsequent promotions or positions.

Alexander, Harold

(1891–1969) Nationality: British.
Senior position: Supreme Allied Commander,
   Mediterranean.
Final rank: Field Marshal.

Anders, Wladyslaw

(1892–1970) Nationality: Polish.
Senior position: Commander-in-Chief, Polish Army.
Final rank: Lieutenant-General.

Alexander took part in the battle for France in 1940. Thereafter he served in Burma and India before transferring to the Middle East in 1942 as the senior British commander. After overseeing the defeat of Axis forces there in spring 1943, he took part in the Sicilian and Italian campaigns.

Above: Alexander (right) confers with British and US staff officers during the campaign in Northwest Europe, 1944-1945.

Anders was captured by the Russians in 1939 but was allowed to leave for Palestine in 1942 after the Russo-German campaign had begun. There he helped form the Polish II Corps, which fought with distinction in Italy, most notably at Monte Cassino.

Above: Anders began the war as commander of a cavalry brigade but by 1945 he was in charge of an army of some 112,000 exiled Poles.

Arnold, Henry

(1886–1950) Nationality: American.
Senior position: Commander General, US Army Air Forces.
Final rank: General of the Army.

Auchinleck, Claude

(1884–1981) Nationality: British.
Senior position: Commander-in-Chief, India.
Final rank: Field Marshal.

An early advocate of air power, "Hap" Arnold spent the entire war in staff posts, directing the expansion and operations of the US Army Air Forces. He served with the US and Allied Joint Chiefs-of-Staff and directed both the Pacific and European strategic bombing offensives.

Above: "Hap" Arnold was in charge of expanding the US Army Air Forces and increased its strength from around 35,000 men in 1935 to a massive two million by 1945.

Auchinleck was a career soldier who saw action in World War I. He was posted to India in the late 1920s and was made chief of the General Staff of the Indian Army in 1936. He returned to England in 1940 to take part in the Anglo-French Narvik operation in Norway that May and then

Above: Affectionately known as the "Auk," Auchinleck was one of the British Army's most respected senior officers but fell foul of Churchill for the loss of Tobruk in 1942.

17

oversaw the beaten force's evacuation the following month. He subsequently returned to India to take command of the British forces stationed there but was soon on the move again—this time to the strategically vital Middle East.

Auchinleck was made commander-in-chief, Middle East in June 1941 and he was fully backed by Churchill but the latter's support ebbed away over the next few months as the former refused to order an attack due to shortages of men and equipment. The fall of Tobruk in January 1942 weakened Auchinleck's position further and, although he redeemed himself considerably with a victory of sorts at the First Battle of El Alamein in June, when Rommel's drive towards Egypt was halted, Auchinleck was replaced by Alexander the next month. He served in India for the remainder of the conflict.

Below: Auchinleck (second from left) inspects military police shortly after his return to England in January 1940, after serving in India since 1927.

Badoglio, Pietro
(1871–1956) Nationality: Italian.
Senior position: Chief-of-Staff.
Final rank: Field Marshal.

During the interwar years Badoglio fought in wars in Africa, served in World War I and led the annexation of Ethiopia in 1936. He was then appointed the army's chief-of-staff on Italy's entry into World War II. He resigned in 1940 over military failure in Greece but re-emerged in 1943 to engineer Mussolini's downfall.

Above: Never a supporter of Mussolini, Badoglio signed the armistice with the Allies in 1943 and went on to become Italy's post-fascist prime minister.

Beck, Ludwig

(1880–1944) Nationality: German.
Senior position: Chief-of-Staff, OKW.
Final rank: General.

Blamey, Thomas

(1884–1951) Nationality: Australian.
Senior position: General Officer Commanding
   Australian Imperial Force.
Final rank: General.

Beck was a careerist officer of no little moral courage who resigned as the chief-of-staff of the *Oberkommando der Wehrmacht* in 1938 in opposition to Hitler's aggressive war plans as he felt they would bring disaster. He was a leading figure among those involved in the July 1944 Bomb Plot, but was captured in Berlin and allowed to commit suicide.

Above: Beck was a German officer of the old school—aristocratic, intellectual, and conservative—and highly principled when it came to opposing Hitler's geopolitical ambitions.

Blamey took charge of the Australian Imperial Force, Middle East, in February 1940 but also fought in Greece. He returned home in March 1942 as commander-in-chief Allied Land Forces and oversaw operations in the Southwest Pacific, notably on New Guinea.

Above: Blamey (right) played a pivotal role in the New Guinea campaign during the twelve months after September 1942, and became the first Australian to hold the rank of field marshal.

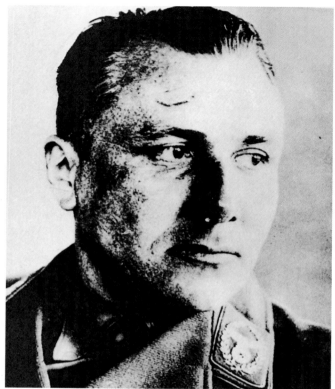

Bock, Fedor von

(1885–1945) Nationality: German.
Senior position: Commander Army Group South.
Final rank: Field Marshal.

An army group commander during the invasions of Poland, Western Europe, and the Soviet Union, Bock was sacked in December 1941 but was recalled in early 1942 to take command of Army Group South. He was removed in July and killed in an Allied air raid while in retirement.

Above: Bock was a career officer but was yet another senior German general who felt Hitler's rage, chiefly because he disagreed with the direction of the war.

Bormann, Martin

(1900–1945) Nationality: German.
Senior position: Secretary to Hitler.

Bormann, a former member of the right-wing paramilitary *Freikorps*, joined the Nazi Party in its early street-fighting days in the 1920s and gradual rose through its ranks, becoming chief-of-staff to deputy leader Hess in 1933 and subsequently the party's national organizer. His great

Above: Although little known among ordinary Germans, Bormann was one of the most important figures in the Nazi hierarchy and controlled access to Hitler.

chance came with the much-debated defection of Hess to Britain in May 1941, whereupon Hitler abolished the post of deputy leader and created in its place the Party Chancellery, a body that Bormann was given.

Bormann was a dedicated Nazi—his first child was named Adolf and Hitler was also his godfather—and, although outwardly seemingly unprepossessing, he became the power behind the throne, denying or permitting access to his master as he saw fit and largely for his own purposes as the Third Reich began to fall apart. He was an arch political operator, one dubbed the "Brown Eminence" by those who dealt with him, and he earned the enmity of many of his colleagues. Loyal to the bitter end, he signed Hitler's final political testament and was a witness to his marriage to Eva Braun in 1945. He was killed while trying to escape from Berlin.

Bradley, Omar

(1893–1981) Nationality: American.
Senior position: Commander US 12th Army Group.
Final rank: General of the Army.

Bradley was a career soldier who graduated from West Point in 1915 and then held various staff and instructor positions in the interwar years. He served on the General

Above: Bormann (left) pictured with other members of the Nazi Party within Hitler's inner circle enjoying a break from his official duties.

Above: Bradley (left) discusses strategy with Eisenhower during the latter stages of the campaign in Northwest Europe, probably in early 1945.

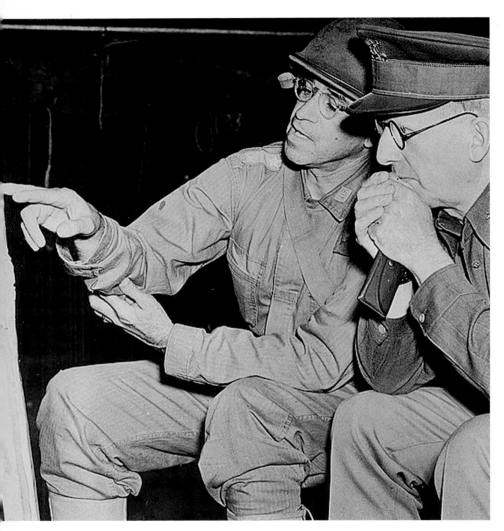

Bradley was then posted to England in September to take part in the buildup to the Normandy landings and in January 1944 was given charge of the US First Army, which was to form the right flank of the D-Day operation. After the Allies had come ashore in occupied France on 6 June, they rapidly became bogged down but Bradley engineered the final break-out, Operation Cobra, that saw the Allies sweep across France in a matter of weeks. He was made commander of the 12th Army Group, a body of 1.3 million men that remains the largest force ever led by a US general officer, the following September.

This army group fought its way across Western Europe until the end of the war in May 1945, with elements taking part in some of the most important battles of the campaign, not least the fighting in the heavily forested Ardennes during the winter of 1944-1945.

Bradley was not of the first rank in terms of pure generalship but he had qualities that were often in short supply among some of his more fractious peers—not least tact and calmness, traits that proved vital in his dealings with both Patton and Montgomery. He was also a superb organizer and planner, skills that proved invaluable during Cobra and the Battle of the Bulge. Bradley also exhibited a genuine and deep-felt compassion for the ordinary soldiers under his command so much so that he became known as the "GI General."

Above: Bradley (left) outlines the progress of his own 12th Army Group during the drive towards the German border in late 1944.

Staff between 1938 and 1941 and as a brigadier at the Infantry School between March 1941 and February

1942. He briefly commanded two divisions preparing for combat but first saw action as commander of the US II Corps, formerly commanded by Patton, in the latter part of the Tunisian campaign in early 1943 and also during the Sicilian campaign of 10 July to 17 August.

Brauchitsch, Walther von

(1881–1948) Nationality: German.
Senior position: Commander-in-
Chief of the German Army.
Final rank: Field Marshal.

Brauchitsch was made commander-in-chief in 1938 and planned the invasions of Poland and Western Europe. He opposed Hitler in the latter case and was reprimanded. Yet he remained in position until December 1941, finally resigning through ill-health. Hitler, although without high command experience, took over Brauchitsch's duties.

Right: Victorious German troops line a boulevard in Paris after marching into the undefended French capital on 14 June 1940.
Below: Brauchitsch (second from right) congratulates one of his officers during the *Blitzkrieg* against France and the Low countries in 1940.

Brereton, Lewis

(1890–1967) Nationality: American.
Senior position: Commander First Allied Airborne Army.
Final rank: Major-General.

Brereton was a long-term advocate of air power. He was serving in the Philippines in 1941 but then transferred to the Middle East and then Europe as commander of what became the US Ninth Air Force. After supporting the Normandy landings in 1944, his airborne army took part in the Arnhem operation and the crossing of the Rhine in March 1945.

Above: Brereton was both resourceful and energetic, but was criticized for his performance during the Japanese invasion of the Philippines and at Arnhem.

Brooke, Alan

(1883–1963) Nationality: British.
Senior position: Chief of the General Staff.
Final rank: Field Marshal.

Brooke is by no means one of the most well known British generals of the war, largely because his exploits on the battlefield were somewhat limited, but his importance to the Allied cause was immense. He did take part in the Battle for France and the Low Countries from May 1940 onwards, when he commanded the British II Corps and, with no small amount of skill, oversaw the tricky evacuation from Dunkirk. The key moment came in late 1941, a particular low low-point in Britain's fortunes, when Dill

Above: Brooke (left) pictured somewhere in southern England shortly before the German invasion of France and the Low Countries in May 1940.

was removed from his position as chief of the General Staff.

Brooke was named his replacement and his new role brought him into almost daily contact with Churchill. Brooke needed all his interpersonal skills to rein in some of his political master's more extreme plans. He invariably kept his frustrations to himself and was exceptionally good at turning Churchill's often fanciful strategic visions into practical military options. He also worked well with his US counterparts but was notably disappointed that he was not made the supreme Allied commander for the Normandy landings.

Budenny, Semyon

(1883–1973) Nationality: Russian.
Senior position: Commander-in-Chief of the Russian
  Armies in the Ukraine and Bessarabia.
Final rank: Marshal of the Soviet Union.

Budenny took charge in the Ukraine and Bessarabia in June 1941 and suffered huge losses during the German *Blitzkrieg*. He was sacked in September but subsequently served as commander-in-chief in the Caucasus and as commander of cavalry.

Above: Brooke (left) looks less than relaxed alongside Eisenhower and Montgomery during the liberation of Northwest Europe, 1944–1945.

Above: Budenny also served in the Russo-Japanese War (1904–1905), World War I (1914–1918), the Russian Civil War (1917–1922), and the Russo-Polish War (1919–1921)

Burke, Arleigh

(1901–1996) Nationality: American.
Senior position: Chief-of-staff to
Mitscher.
Final rank: Captain.

Burke was an aggressive commander of destroyers, who in May 1943 was given charge of Destroyer Squadron 23. He fought in more than twenty engagements and showed considerable aggression before serving in the Battles of the Philippines Sea and Leyte Gulf in 1944 as a member of Mitscher's staff.

Left: Burke was renowned for how quickly he was able to engage the Japanese, so much so that he was dubbed "31 Knot Burke" by a senior commander.

Busch, Ernst von

(1885–1945) Nationality: German.
Senior position: Commander Army
Group Center.
Final rank: Field Marshal.

Busch was given command of the Sixteenth Army in 1938 and oversaw its operations in Poland, Western Europe, and the Soviet Union. He commanded an army group on the Eastern Front from October 1943 to June 1944 but was then replaced by Model. He served in northern Europe from March 1945 but died in British captivity after the war.

Below: Busch (right) among a German envoy meeting Montgomery, having agreed the terms of surrender.

Chamberlain, Neville
(1869–1940) Nationality: British.
Senior position: Prime Minister.

Chennault, Claire
(1890–1958) Nationality: American.
Senior position: Commander US 14th Army Air Force.
Final rank: Major-General.

Chamberlain, a conservative, became leader in 1937 and was concerned with keeping the peace in Europe. He was outmaneuvered by Hitler and Mussolini, saw Czechoslovakia dismembered, and only belatedly stood up to the fascist foe. Hopelessly compromised and severely ill, he resigned in 1940 and was replaced by Churchill.

Above: Much castigated for his failed diplomatic dealings with Hitler, Chamberlain resigned on 10 May 1940, the day the Germans launched their *Blitzkrieg*.

Chennault came to prominence after raising the all-volunteer Flying Tigers fighter unit to fight in Burma during 1941, but in 1942 took command of the 14th Army Air Force in China. This was such a threat that the Japanese launched a partially successful offensive against its bases. Chennault resigned over policy in mid-1945.

Above: Chennault (in leather jacket) talks to ground crew working on a US fighter, part of the US 14th Army Air Force based in China.

Chuikov, Vasili

(1900–1982) Nationality: Russian.
Senior position: Commander Eighth Guards Army.
Final rank: General.

Chuikov served in the Soviet Ministry of War between 1941 and 1942 but was given command of the beleaguered Sixty-second Army at Stalingrad and effectively stopped the city from falling. His command was later redesignated the Eighth Guards Army, which served with distinction for the remainder of the war.

Above: Chuikov (right) led the heroic defense of Stalingrad and was one of the Red Army's most able field commanders of the war.

Churchill, Winston

(1874–1965)
Nationality: British.
Senior position: Prime Minister.

Although Churchill had held several senior political positions in World War I, including that of first lord of the Admiralty and minister of munitions, he spent a sizeable part of the interwar years in the political wilderness and supplemented his income by writing at length on various, often historical subjects. He remained a member of parliament for much of the 1930s but held no cabinet post and was chiefly known for his vocal and persistent support for

Below: With characteristic belligerence, Churchill checks over a Tommy gun after the evacuation from Dunkirk, 1940.

Above: Churchill inspects British troops in the Western Desert, after the defeat of France.

rearmament and his opposition to appeasing Nazi Germany at a time when neither was a popular position to adopt.

Churchill's fortunes changed dramatically when Britain declared war on Germany on 3 September 1940 after the latter had invaded Poland. He was recalled as first lord of the

Admiralty by the ailing and increasingly discredited Chamberlain and became prime minister in his stead when the latter resigned. He took up the post on 10 May—the day Germany invaded France and the Low Countries—and was soon head of a coalition government. Within a few months, Britain was effectively fighting alone and it was now that Churchill displayed the fortitude, strength of character, and outstanding oratorical skills —at least in public; in

private he was prone to periods of self-doubt and deep depression—that made him the consummate wartime leader.

Victory in the Battle of Britain in the late summer insured Britain's survival, although the ongoing Battle of the Atlantic caused him many worries for much of the remainder of the war. Churchill sought to strike back as best he could with the extremely limited resources at his command. He ordered commando

Above: The British prime minister maintains the bulldog spirit even in a more formal pose.

supplies would, thanks to the expansion of Lend-Lease, soon turn into a torrent. Churchill and Roosevelt, who corresponded and spoke frequently, had a cordial relationship and concluded the Atlantic Charter, a blueprint for peace and the post-war world, during meeting in Newfoundland's Placentia Bay in August 1941.

The two, along with other Allied leaders, would have further conferences but as the war progressed it became apparent that Churchill and Roosevelt had somewhat different priorities and the latter was somewhat the junior partner in the relationship. Churchill's world view was largely dominated by his concerns over the future of the British Empire and the nature of the postwar world, while Roosevelt's first concern was to win the war and then define the precise nature of the peace. Churchill did, nevertheless, made some correct strategic suggestions, such as postponing any cross-Channel invasion in 1942 and 1943, but often for the wrong reasons. He preferred the indirect approach and this led to the Italian campaign that tied up considerable resources that would have been more fruitfully deployed elsewhere. The simple truth was that Italy's surrender in 1943 did not bring about Germany's collapse and Churchill was wrong to believe that it would.

Despite such errors of judgment, there is absolutely no doubt that Churchill was Britain's savior during the war and huge crowds that had gathered outside Buckingham Palace

raids, early strategic bombing missions over Europe, and larger military campaigns in the peripheral theaters, chiefly in the Mediterranean where the protection of the Suez Canal was a priority. Better news came in July 1941, when Nazi Germany invaded the Soviet Union. Churchill and Stalin were hardly ideological bedfellows but the former took the view that "my enemy's enemy is my friend" and was content

enough to see the greater part of Hitler's war machine directed elsewhere.

Salvation really came in December 1941. The Japanese attacked Pearl Harbor on the 7th and Hitler declared war on the United States four days later. Churchill had long been cultivating Roosevelt as a potential ally but the latter had had to tread a fine political line since popular US feeling was broadly isolationist before Pearl Harbor. He had nevertheless been gradually increasingly US aid to Britain during its period of isolation and this trickle of

to cheer him and the royal family after the defeat of Germany in May 1945 were clear evidence of his towering statesmanship. Yet the prime minister, who was held in enormous affection, was voted out of office the following

Above: The "Big Three"—Churchill, Roosevelt, and Stalin—pictured at the Yalta Conference, which was held between 4-11 February 1945. With victory in sight, their discussions largely centered on the shape of the postwar world.

31

July. This was not a reflection on his wartime leadership but rather a reflection of a popular clamor, after years of hardship, for a peace dividend. Churchill was perceived as an unequalled war leader but not the prime minister to devise and push through reform that in anyway matched the widespread social legislation that was being mooted by the rival Labour Party.

Below: Churchill takes center stage in a propaganda poster issued when Britain stood alone against the might of Nazi Germany.

Ciano, Galeazzo
(1903–1944) Nationality: Italian.
Senior position: Foreign Minister.

This diplomat's marriage to Mussolini's daughter saw him rapidly promoted to foreign minister in 1936. He signed the Pact of Steel with Germany in 1939 but was opposed to war. He resigned in 1943 and backed Mussolini's removal. Ciano was captured by the Germans the following year and executed.

Above: As Hitler looks on in the background, Ciano signs the document that tied Italy ever closer to Nazi Germany, a political development that he largely opposed.

Clark, Mark

(1896–1984) Nationality: American.
Senior position: Commander 15th
Army Group.
Final rank: General.

Clark was a careerist soldier who had served and been wounded on the Western Front during World War I. In the interwar years he attended infantry school and the Army War College, and in 1940 he became an instructor at the latter institution, where he became involved in the ongoing expansion of the US Army. Following US entry into the war, he was made chief-of-staff of Army Ground Forces in May 1942 but transferred to Europe as commander of US forces in Britain the following July. Clark now began to take on more active roles.

He was involved in delicate negotiations with the Vichy French authorities in North Africa during October that were part of the preparations for Operation Torch, the Anglo-American landings in North Africa. During the actual operation in November he served under Eisenhower as his commander of Allied forces in North Africa and from January 1943, as commander of the Fifth Army, he began preparations for the invasion of Italy. His army came

Right: A studio portrait of Clark when he was a two-star general. He wears the shoulder badge of the Army Ground Forces, US-based troops engaged in training, supplying or supporting roles.

Above: Clark, now a three-star general, talks to various Allied officers. His shoulder patch is that of the 15th Army Group in Italy, which he took over in late 1944.

ashore at Salerno the following September and only narrowly avoided being thrown back into the sea.

Clark next led his forces up the western side of the Italian peninsula in a costly, slow-moving campaign that ground to a halt beneath Monte Cassino. A gamble to break this deadlock that involved landing part of the Fifth Army at Anzio in January 1944 was an out-and-out failure. When the troops in the beachhead finally broke out, thanks to the fall of Cassino to the south, Clark raced north to capture Rome on 4 June, rather than driving directly across the peninsula to trap the German troops retreating from Cassino. It was a controversial decision that put publicity—Rome was the first Axis city liberated by the Allies—above

military need.

Clark next pushed across the River Arno and then north to the formidable Gothic Line. Made commander of the Anglo-American 15th Army Group in December 1944, he oversaw its operations that broke the Gothic Line and cleared the valley of the River Po, and saw its units established in Austria by the end of the fighting in May 1945.

Collins, Joseph

(1896–1963) Nationality: American.
Senior position: Commander US VII Corps.
Final rank: Major-General.

"Lightnin' Joe" first saw service as a commander in the Pacific during 1942 and 1943 but in December 1943 took command of the US VII Corps in Europe. This landed at Utah Beach on D-Day in 1944, fought all the way through Western Europe, and linked up with Soviet forces on the River Elbe in 1945.

Coningham, Arthur

(1895–1948) Nationality: New Zealander.
Senior position: Commander 2nd Tactical Air Force.
Final rank: Air Marshal.

Nicknamed "Maori," Coningham was given charge of the RAF's No. 4 Bomber Group in England in 1939 but became renowned as commander of the Western Desert Air Force. He later led all the British and US air forces in Tunisia and the Anglo-Canadian 2nd Tactical Air Force in Western Europe from July 1944 until the war's end.

Left: Collins was nicknamed "Lightnin' Joe" after the lightning bolt shoulderpatch of the 25th Infantry Division he commanded in the Southwest Pacific.

Crerar, Henry

(1888–1965) Nationality: Canadian.
Senior position: Commander 21st Army Group.
Final rank: General.

Cunningham, Alan

(1887–1983) Nationality: British.
Senior position: Commander Eighth Army.
Final rank: Lieutenant-General.

Crerar was closely involved in the buildup of Canadian forces in Britain from 1940 but resigned to command I Canadian Corps, which fought in Sicily. In 1943 he was recalled to lead the 1st Canadian Army, which fought across Western Europe from 1944 to 1945. From February he commanded a 500,000-plus army group.

Above: Crerar boards a light aircraft to attend an Allied meeting during his army's drive along the coast of northern France in 1944.

Cunningham liberated Ethiopia from Italian rule during 1940 and 1941 and in August 1941 transferred to the Western Desert to take charge of the Eighth Army. He failed to relieve besieged Tobruk, lost the confidence of his superiors, and was replaced in November. Thereafter he served in various administrative roles.

Above: Younger brother of a successful admiral, Cunningham joined the army and liberated Ethiopia from the Italians.

Cunningham, Andrew

(1883–1963) Nationality: British.
Senior position: First Sea Lord.
Final rank: Admiral.

Curtin, John

(1885–1945) Nationality: Australian.
Senior position: Prime Minister.

Cunningham made his name when commander-in-chief of the British Mediterranean Fleet, scoring notable victories at Taranto in 1940 and Matapan in 1941, but his warships suffered heavy losses during the evacuation of Crete. After a spell in Washington, he planned the North African and Sicily landings, and undertook desk duties from late 1943.

Above: Cunningham, Britain's best fighting admiral, was made first sea lord, largely an administrative position, in late 1943.

Curtin served as prime minister from 1941 until shortly before the war's end. Although he was initially an opponent of conscription, he backed it from December 1941 and, despite Churchill's opposition, set about realigning his foreign policy towards the United States rather than Britain. Weakened by illness, he died in July 1945.

Above: Curtin had an uneasy relationship with Churchill, chiefly over naval support in the Far East.

Daladier, Edouard
(1884–1974) Nationality: French.
Senior position: Prime Minister.

Darlan, Jean
(1881–1942) Nationality: French.
Senior position: Commander-in-Chief French Navy.
Final rank: Admiral.

This radical socialist signed the Munich Agreement in 1938 but gradually lost the confidence of his supporters and the French people. His government collapsed in March 1940 but he remained minister of national defense. Later captured in Vichy North Africa, he spent the remainder of the war imprisoned in Germany.

Above: Daladier on trial at Riom, where he was charged by the Vichy French authorities of leading France into a war unprepared.

After France's defeat Darlan sent his fleet to Vichy North Africa, where a large part was destroyed by the British in July 1940. He thereafter became vice-premier in the Vichy government but in 1942 he returned to North Africa and began to curry favor with the US authorities. He was, however, assassinated by a compatriot on Christmas Eve.

Above: Darlan arranged a ceasefire with the Allies in France's North Africa colonies, leading the Germans to occupy Vichy France and Tunisia.

De Gaulle, Charles

(1890–1970) Nationality: French.
Senior position: Free French leader.
Final rank: General.

De Gaulle served as a junior officer during World War I, being wounded and taken prisoner during the Battle of Verdun in 1916. During the interwar era he gained something of a reputation as a military thinker and an ardent supporter of armored warfare. His efforts were belatedly rewarded on 11 May 1940, when he was given command of the inexperienced and hardly combat ready French 4th Armored Division. The army performed badly during the Battle for France but de Gaulle showed some spirit and enjoyed a small measure of success during the

Above: De Gaulle converses with an official from Gabon, which was captured by Free French forces in mid-November 1940.
Left: The crowning moment of de Gaulle's wartime career was his triumphant entry into Paris on 26 August 1944. Here, French troops parade past ecstatic crowds.

fighting around Montcornet later in the month. He was made under-secretary for war but, with the cause lost in his homeland, de Gaulle went into British exile on 17 June.

The next day he made a radio broadcast to his fellow countrymen, stating that the war would go on and that he was the head of what was dubbed "Free France." The call had little immediate impact, not least

Above: In mid-July 1944 De Gaulle speaks from the balcony of the town hall of Bayeaux, announcing the creation of a new French government-in-waiting.

because the French public were coming to terms with imminent defeat and there still was, in name at least, a government in France. De Gaulle was branded a traitor by some. He did, however, gain Churchill's backing, and attempted to gain control of his country's colonies, although an attack on Dakar in October was a disaster and an invasion of Syria in June 1941 was fiercely resisted by the local French forces.

Matters improved as the puppet Vichy French government began to openly side with the Nazis, and De Gaulle gradually established himself as the head of a legitimate government in exile. He finally returned to his native soil on 13 June 1944 and his triumph was sealed when he walked through the center of Paris to widespread popular acclaim on 25 August. He was named president and head of the Committee of National Liberation but was somewhat shunned by the western Allies and not invited to various conferences. It was a slight that he would find difficult to forgive when he attempted to reassert France's status as a world power.

De Guingand, Francis

(1900–1970) Nationality: British.
Senior position: Chief-of-Staff to
Montgomery.
Final rank: Major-General.

De Guingand was a staff officer of great ability and served with Montgomery during the campaigns in North Africa and Western Europe. He was an expert negotiator, often representing Montgomery in various meetings, and was able to smooth the sometimes difficult relations between his boss and Eisenhower.

De Lattre de Tassigny, Jean

(1889–1952) Nationality: French.
Senior position: Commander First
Army.
Final rank: General.

De Lattre de Tassigny was a dedicated careerist soldier who was sent to Tunisia by the Vichy government but began to express anti-German and pro-Allied sympathies. Recalled home, he was imprisoned after making anti-German statements but escaped in 1943 and subsequently led the First Army in North Africa and Western Europe.

Right: De Lattre de Tassigny signed Germany's surrender document on behalf of France in May 1945.

Dempsey, Miles
(1896–1969) Nationality: British.
Senior position: Commander Second Army.
Final rank: Lieutenant-General.

Devers, Jacob
(1887–1979) Nationality: American.
Senior position: Commander Sixth Army Group.
Final rank: General.

Dempsey, who fought at Dunkirk, was then tasked with raising an armored division. Thereafter he successfully led the British XIII Corps in latter stages of the North African campaign, in Sicily, and then Italy. He was next given the Second Army, which fought in Western Europe from 1944 to 1945.

Above: Dempsey (center) and Churchill discuss progress of Second Army in Northwest Europe, while Montgomery looks on.

Devers held senior staff posts from May 1943 to October 1944 as the US Army's commander of European Theater of Operations, and then the African Theater of Operations, and finally as Allied commander in the Mediterranean. He then led the Sixth Army Group from southern France into southern Germany and then on to Austria.

Above: Devers' army group in southern France and Germany consisted of the US Seventh Army and the French Second Army.

Doenitz, Karl

(1891–1980) Nationality: German.
Senior position: Commander-in-Chief Germany Navy.
Final rank: Admiral.

Doentiz served aboard Germany's U-boats during World War I and stayed in the much-reduced navy during the interwar years, even though it had been prohibited by the Treaty of Versailles to have submarines. A keen proponent of undersea warfare, he was made commander of the country's small submarine force, which was being revitalized amid considerable secrecy in 1935, and oversaw its gradual but not insignificant expansion in the years before the outbreak of war. He was made rear admiral in October 1939 and was ordered to conduct a campaign against Allied shipping with the limited resources he had available. Doenitz began to lobby hard for more resources and an expansion of the submarine fleet, a position that brought him into direct conflict with more conservative senior naval officers, such as the commander-in-chief, Raeder, who wanted to emphasize the importance of surface warships.

Hilter gradually lost faith in the navy's surface fleet when it suffered a series of losses, like that of the *Bismarck* in 1941, and Doenitz began to prosper thanks to the growing number of Allied merchant ships being sent to the bottom by his submariners. He was promoted vice-admiral in 1940 and full admiral in 1942 and finally replaced the discredited Raeder in January 1943. The surface fleet was all but moribund by this juncture and, henceforth, the navy's expanding force of U-boats bore the brunt of the vital Battle of the

Above: Doenitz (right) was an outstanding naval commander and was one of the few military men that Hitler trusted in the final

Atlantic. Yet by the end of the year, the Allies had turned a corner and had the upper hand in the Atlantic.

Doenitz tried to regain the initiative with new tactics, equipment, and submarines but the battle had been largely lost and his U-boat fleet was gradually ground down during the remainder of the campaign. Hitler made Doenitz his successor as chancellor in his will of 30 April 1945 but Doenitz ruled the fast-disintegrating Third Reich for little more than a week before "negotiating" its surrender. Tried at Nuremberg, he was convicted of war crimes and served ten years, being released in 1956.

Above: Doenitz pictured on an inspection tour of one of the main U-boat bases on the west coast of France at the height of the Battle of the Atlantic.

Right: The crew of one of Doenitz's U-boats load a torpedo—a tricky and delicate operation—before beginning a sortie into the North Sea.

Doolittle, James

(1896–1958) Nationality: American.
Senior position: Commander-in-
Chief Eighth Army Air Force.
Final rank: Lieutenant-General.

Doolittle grabbed the headlines for launching a dramatic bombing raid on Japan in April 1942. He then transferred to England to take charge of the US Twelfth Army Air Force, which fought in North Africa and the Mediterranean. He returned to England to command the Eighth from January 1944 to May 1945, and then served in the Pacific.

Above: One of the sixteen B-25 bombers deployed on the Doolittle Raid takes off from the deck of the aircraft carrier *Hornet* on 18 April 1942.
Left: Doolittle was a colonel at the time of the raid.

45

Douglas, William

(1893–1969) Nationality: British.
Senior position: Commander-in-Chief RAF Fighter
Command/Coastal Command.
Final rank: Air Marshal.

Douglas was assistant chief of the Air Staff in 1939 but was made head of the RAF's Fighter Command in late 1940 and held the post until 1943, when he transferred to the RAF's Middle East Command. He was given charge of RAF Coastal Command in early 1944 and was involved in D-Day and the Battle of the Atlantic.

Right: Douglas was a World War I fighter ace and briefly served as a commercial pilot before rejoining the Royal Air Force in 1920.
Below: Douglas pictured studying a war document.

Dowding, Hugh

(1882–1970) Nationality: British.
Senior position: Commander-in-Chief RAF Fighter
Command.
Final rank: Air Chief Marshal.

Dowding began his long military career as a second lieutenant in the artillery, serving in India and the Far East from 1900 to 1910, but became interested in the very new art of military aviation after a two-year spell at military college had ended in 1912. He gained his flying certificate the same year and moved to the Royal Flying Corps in 1914. During World War I he served in various staff positions and remained in what was by the end of the conflict the Royal Air Force during the interwar years. He commanded No. 1 Group in southern England from 1922 until 1925 and then spent part of the decade serving overseas and in more staff positions.

Dowding served on the Air Council for Research and Development from 1930 until 1936, and this proved a key posting as he became a staunch backer of those wishing to build better fighters, chiefly the Spitfire, and develop new technologies such as radar at a time when military spending was a relatively low priority. He was given charge of Fighter Command in July 1936 and immediately instigated a root-and-branch reform with an emphasis on organization and communications that, along with radar and new fighters, would greatly contribute to the outnumbered Fighter Command's eventual victory in the Battle of Britain in 1940. His efforts were just in time.

Dowding, known as "Stuffy" behind his back, was not an easy man to like as he lacked the humor and personality traits that would have endeared him to his colleagues and political superiors, but his plan for fighting the Battle of Britain, the first great air campaign in history, were virtually flawless given the resources he had to hand—a lack of fully trained pilots was a constant worry. Yet he never enjoyed the fruits of victory or much popular acclaim and seems not to have met with Churchill's approval. He was replaced on 18 November 1940 and spent a little time serving

with the Ministry for Aircraft Production delegation to the United States before retiring in 1942.

Above: Dowding tightly controlled the Battle of Britain and made careful use of his scarce resources to achieve a critical victory.

Eaker, Ira

(1898–1987) Nationality: American.
Senior position: Commander-in-Chief
  Mediterranean Allied Air Forces.
Final rank: Lieutenant-General.

Eaker was an advocate of strategic bombing. He took command of the US Eighth Army Air Force in eastern England from December 1942 and convinced his political masters of the need to bomb Germany in strength. He transferred to the Mediterranean in January 1944 and served there until the war's end.

Left: Eaker was one of those who devised the combined bomber offensive against Germany.

Eden, Anthony

(1897–1977) Nationality: British.
Senior position: Foreign Minister.

Eden resigned as foreign secretary in Chamberlain's government in 1938 but was recalled when Britain went to war, serving first as Dominion secretary and then as secretary of state for war. Churchill made him his foreign secretary in 1940 and he held the post until 1945.

Left: As British foreign secretary, Eden (standing behind Churchill) attended virtually all of the major Allied conferences during the war—this is Yalta in early 1945—and was generally recognized within the political establishment as Churchill's successor if anything happened to the latter.

Eichelberger, Robert

(1886–1961) Nationality: American.
Senior position: Commander Eighth Army.
Final rank: Lieutenant-General.

Eichmann, Adolf

(1906–1962) Nationality: German.
Senior position: Head of the Gestapo's Department of
Jewish Affairs.
Final rank: Lieutenant-Colonel.

Eichelberger took charge of a US corps in 1942 and was tasked with halting the Japanese advance through New Guinea towards Australia. He won a notable victory at Buna in early 1943 and in September 1944 was given an army for the landings in the Philippines. He was made commander of all occupying ground forces in Japan in January 1946.

Above: Eichelberger became an expert on amphibious landings and took part in a staggering fifty-two operations, mostly in the Southwest Pacific, during the war.

Eichmannn was the SS officer who, after the infamous Wannsee Conference of early 1942, became one of the key figures in the implementation of the anti-Jewish genocide known as the "Final Solution." He vanished in 1945 but was discovered in South America in 1960. Kidnapped by Israel agents, Eichmann was put on trial and hanged.

Above: SS officer Adolf Eichmann, often referred to as "the architect of the Holocaust."

Eisenhower, Dwight

(1890–1969) Nationality: American.
Senior position: Supreme
Commander of the Allied
Expeditionary Force.
Final rank: General of the Army.

Above: A formal photograph of Eisenhower taken sometime after December 1944, when he was promoted to the rank of general of the army, as indicated by the insignia on his epaulettes.

Eisenhower, who came from a relatively impoverished background, graduated from West Point academy in 1915 and served in various training capacities during US participation in World War I. For the next two decades or so, he served overseas in Panama (1922-1924) and the Philippines (1935-1939), but also attended the Command and General Staff School and the Army War College in the late 1920s. He also had an assignment to the office of the chief-of-staff to MacArthur. Eisenhower was promoted to the rank of brigadier-general in late 1941, largely for his excellent performance as the chief-of-staff to the US Third Army during that summer's maneuvers. His good work was noted by Marshall, chief-of-staff to the US Army, who marked him out for greater things despite his patent lack of combat or high command experience.

When war broke out in the Pacific in December 1941 he was assistant chief of the Army War Plans Division, but thereafter served overseas. In June 1942, shortly after promotion to major-general, Eisenhower was made head of the European Theater of Operations and commander of all the US forces in Europe. His first active role the following November was to take charge of Operation Torch, the successful Anglo-American landings in French North Africa. From then until May 1943, he directed the sometimes fraught campaign in Tunisia that was the springboard for the invasion of Sicily (July-August), followed by the initial landings on the Italian mainland during September and October.

In late November Eisenhower left the Mediterranean theater for the last time and traveled to England to prepare for what would become Operation Overlord, the invasion of Europe. The next month he was made supreme commander of the Allied Expeditionary Force that was tasked with the liberation of occupied Western Europe. Overlord, a highly complex operation, was largely an unqualified successes but the breakout from Normandy proved much more difficult. It finally came on 25 July and by mid-September the Allies, who had been advancing on a broad front as advocated by Eisenhower, were knocking at the gates of Germany at certain points.

Eisenhower, who had been given

Below: Eisenhower drives home a point during a discussion with a member of the 101st Airborne Division shortly before D-Day.

direct control of operations on 1 September, had problems—the Allied supply lines were increasingly overstretched and winter was fast approaching. Two of his most fractious generals, Montgomery and Patton, both offered to end the war with a narrow-front offensive and, after some soul-searching, he reluctantly agreed a concession. The broad-front strategy would continue come what may, but Montgomery's plan would be allowed to go ahead. This was the risky, overly ambitious Arnhem operation that called for a very narrow thrust into the Ruhr, Germany's industrial heartland, in

late September to finish the war quickly.

It was a considerable failure and the supreme commander had hardly recovered from its aftermath when he faced another serious crisis—the German winter offensive through the wooded Ardennes in Belgium, which opened on 16 December. After overcoming the initial confusion sparked by this surprise attack, Eisenhower's response was precise and ultimately decisive. He rushed US and British troops to the flanks or shoulders of the "bulge" to stop it growing any further and then launched counterattacks that finally

eradicated the threat in late January 1945.

Eisenhower then went over to the offensive and the Allies, with their supply difficulties now behind them, began their final push into Nazi Germany the following month. Operation Varsity, which opened on 7 March, saw them safely across the

Below: Eisenhower (center, front row) poses for a formal photograph with a number of his senior commanders in Europe, including Patton, commander of the US Third Army (second from left, front row), and Bradley, commander of US 12th Army Group (on Eisenhower's left)

River Rhine and thereafter they drove deep into western and southern Germany in the face of crumbling enemy resistance until the official surrender was concluded in early May. The supreme commander remained in Europe as the head of the Allied occupation force until the following November.

Eisenhower's career in World War II was remarkable. He effectively came from nowhere in the military hierarchy to take charge of Anglo-American operations from November 1942 until the end of the war, despite having been personally involved in no more than divisional maneuvers in peacetime. He was promoted over the heads of generals who had had some combat experience, yet the choice was a wise decision and arguably the most militarily important one of the war for the western Allies. They got a supreme commander of outstanding ability and great charm. Informally known as "Ike," Eisenhower was a great organizer and capable of seeing the wider picture but, above all, he was a diplomat with excellent man-management skills. With fiery, mutually antagonistic generals like Montgomery and Patton under his command, Eisenhower needed these latter two traits probably more than any others.

Above: Eisenhower (right) wears the shoulder badge of the SHAEF (Supreme Headquarters Allied Expeditionary Force), the body formed in February 1944 that controlled Allied forces in Northwest Europe.

Falkenhausen, Alexander von

(1878–1966) Nationality: German.
Senior position: Commander-in-Chief France and Belgium.
Final rank: General.

Falkenhausen headed the German forces occupying France and Belgium but his anti-Nazi sympathies became more and more evident from 1942 onwards. His efforts to win supporters to the Bomb Plot failed and he was dismissed in July 1944. Falkenhausen was arrested and imprisoned but survived the war.

Right: Falkenhausen stands trial for his part in the July Bomb Plot—he was sent to Dachau but survived.

Falkenhorst, Nikolaus

(1885–1968) Nationality: German.
Senior position: Commander-in-Chief Norway.
Final rank: Colonel-General.

Falkenhorst carried out the invasion of Norway in 1940 and remained there until 1944. His troops saw little further action, save for a limited invasion of the Soviet Union in 1941, but he was widely hated by the locals for his brutal occupation policies. He was condemned to death after the war but the sentence was commuted.

Right: Falkenhorst inspects just a small fraction of the large German force that garrisoned Norway.

Fitch, Aubrey
(1883–1978) Nationality: American.
Senior position: Commander Task Force 11.
Final rank: Rear-Admiral.

Fletcher, Frank
(1885–1973) Nationality: American.
Senior position: Commander Task Force 17.
Final rank: Vice-Admiral.

Fitch commanded a task force centered on the carrier *Lexington* at the Battle of the Coral Sea in 1942 and aircraft from the latter damaged two Japanese carriers on the last day of the action. *Lexington* was also damaged and eventually lost. Fitch became head of land-based aircraft in the South Pacific.

Above: A studio portrait of Fitch, who led the US effort at the Battle of the Coral Sea in May 1942.

"Black Jack" Fletcher, a career sailor who was awarded the Medal of Honor in 1914, was the main tactical commander at the Battle of the Coral Sea in 1942, despite having little experience of such warships. Aircraft from the carrier *Yorktown* in his Task Force 17 sank one Japanese carrier and damaged another, although the US carrier also took

Above: Fletcher, nicknamed "Black Jack," was deemed overly cautious by some during the early naval battles in the Pacific.

considerable damage. This was in fact quickly repaired and Fletcher was again present as the tactical commander at Midway the following June, directing the combat until *Yorktown* was severely damaged by bombs early in the battle.

He next commanded the three-carrier task force earmarked to protect the landings on Guadalcanal, but left the area of operations early in a much-criticized move ostensibly because of the threat posed by land-based Japanese aircraft. Fletcher fought an inconclusive battle with a Japanese force in the Eastern Solomons in August, although his aircraft did sink the *Ryujo*. He was then given charge of the North Pacific Area of operations in December 1943 and remained in this comparative backwater until the end of the war, whereupon he oversaw the occupation of northern Japan.

Forrestal, James
(1892–1949) Nationality: American.
Senior position: Secretary of the Navy.

Forrestal began his career in Roosevelt's administration in 1940 when he was employed as an administrative assistant, but his rise to prominence was somewhat meteoric. He was promoted to under-secretary of the navy in August and oversaw much of its expansion. He began a new building program as the war clouds gathered and prioritized the allocation of vital resources through the Controlled Materials Plan. This was remarkably successful—the US Navy grew from 1,099 warships to 50,759 over the next three years. He was also instrumental in setting up the Lend-Lease system, traveling to London to discuss its details in 1941.

He was made secretary to the navy in April 1944, in which capacity he visited both the European and Pacific fronts, and even landed on Iwo Jima a mere two days after the initial landings in February 1945.

Forrestal remained active immediately after the war, dealing with postwar reconstruction and devising institutions to deal with the outbreak of the Cold War. He also

successfully prevented the amalgamation of the army, air force, and navy. All of this took its toll and Forrestal went into a destructive downward cycle. He was dismissed in early 1949 and died on 22 May, apparently by suicide although controversy still surrounds his death.

Above: Forrestal waits to take off from Honolulu in the Hawaiian Islands. He became the first secretary of the navy in May 1944.

Franco, Francisco

(1892–1975) Nationality: Spanish.
Senior position: Spanish Nationalist
    Leader.
Final rank: General.

Franco masterminded the army uprising against the legitimately elected
Republican government, sparking the
Spanish Civil War in 1936, and his
eventual victory three years later was

Right: Franco pictured later in life—he
remained in office until his death.
Below: Hitler and Franco meet at Hendaye
in southwest France in October 1940. The
Spanish dictator refused to formally side with
the Axis powers.

in no small measure due to the military aid, chiefly the aircraft of the Condor Legion, dispatched to him by fellow fascist Hitler. The latter and, indeed, many others expected that Franco would reciprocate and side with the Axis powers when World War II began, but this proved not to be the case.

Hitler and Nazi diplomats had several meetings with the dictator, not least at Hendaye on the French-Spanish border in late 1940, to discuss the matter, but Franco kept his much-weakened and war-ravaged country out of the war. The Spanish leader was a hard negotiator and Hitler remarked that he would rather visit the dentist that hold further discussions with him. Later meetings between the countries' diplomats proved equally fruitless but Franco did, however, permit the so-called Blue Division, a force of "volunteer" anti-communists, to fight on the Eastern Front—albeit with little impact.

Freyberg, Bernard

(1889–1963) Nationality: New Zealander.
Senior position: Commander-in-Chief New Zealand Forces.
Final rank: General.

Freyberg first saw action during the invasion of Greece in 1941. He and his troops were withdrawn to Crete, where they put up stiff but finally unsuccessful resistance when the island was invaded that May. He was sent to Egypt and next served in Italy as a corps commander. His men fought at Monte Cassino before ending the war in Trieste.

Above: Freyberg actually trained to be a dentist but spent World War II leading New Zealand troops, and thus commanded one of the best Allied combat formations of the entire war.

Galland, Adolf

(1912–1996) Nationality: German.
Senior position: Commander-in-Chief Luftwaffe
  Fighters.
Final rank: Major-General.

Ghormley, Robert

(1883–1958) Nationality: American.
Senior position: Commander South Pacific Area.
Final rank: Vice-Admiral.

Galland held a *Luftwaffe* staff position during the 1939 invasion of Poland. He took an active command during the attack on France and the Low Countries and participated in the Battle of Britain. He was made commander of the *Luftwaffe*'s fighter arm in 1941 but was dismissed in 1945, after which he commanded a jet fighter unit.

Above: Galland (right) photographed talking to Goering and other senior *Luftwaffe* officers in northern France in 1940.

Ghormley served as the US naval commander in the South Pacific from March 1942 and was tasked with the landings on Guadalcanal. They were dogged by problems and he compounded them by deciding to withdraw supporting carriers shortly after the invasion. He was replaced in November but then held various staff positions in Hawaii and Europe.

Above: Ghormley (center) had one final mission during the war— overseeing the decommissioning of the German Navy in May 1945.

Giraud, Henri

(1879–1949) Nationality: French.
Senior position: Commander-in-Chief French Army.
Final rank: General.

Goebbels, Josef

(1897–1945) Nationality: German.
Senior position: Minister of Propaganda.

Giraud was captured by the Germans in 1940 but managed to escape in 1942. He was courted by the Allies, who initially saw him as a more viable leader of the Free French than de Gaulle. Giraud went to Algiers in November and became the commander of the French Army the following month but was outmaneuvered by de Gaulle and stepped down in 1944.

Above: Giraud (left) resigned when his position as commander-in-chief of the Free French forces was abolished in April 1944.

Goebbels, an early supporter of the Nazis from 1924, was the party's main propagandist as it struggled to win power. Once this had been achieved, he was made its propaganda minister, a post he held continuously from 1933 to 1945. Something of an intellectual heavyweight compared with many of the others in the top echelons of the party, Goebbels proved adept at media manipulation, especially appreciating the power of mass communications and lavish spectacles, such as marches and parades.

Nor was he against lying to achieve his aims—he even

Left: Goebbels was a superb orator and had tight control over the Nazi propaganda machine.

attributed his own limp, which was caused by infantile paralysis, to various causes, from a wound suffered in World War I to a spell in harsh confinement. Nevertheless, he was an expert and powerful orator but one who also recognized the growing importance of modern media, such as film, radio, and television. He was made the guardian of Nazi culture by establishing the Reich Chamber of Culture, which effectively controlled artistic life throughout Nazi Germany.

Yet for all his importance, Goebbels' propaganda effort waned after the outbreak of war. His attempts to undermined British morale through such broadcasts failed entirely, and it even became difficult to main the air of triumphalism on the home front after the disaster at Stalingrad. Goebbels responded by galvanizing the German people into defending their homeland, calling for total war, and took time to take the message directly to heavily bombed cities, something that Hitler never did. He was rewarded by being made "plenipotentiary for total war" in 1944 and remained the loyal Nazi to the bitter end. He, his wife and their six children joined Hitler in his Berlin bunker in the final days of the Third Reich, but on 1 May, the parents first poisoned their children, and then Goebbels shot his wife before turning the gun on himself. Their bodies were taken outside and incinerated

Goering, Hermann

(1893–1946) Nationality: German.
Senior position: Commander-in-Chief Luftwaffe.
Final rank: Reichsmarshall (but stripped of rank 1945).

Goering was a World War I fighter ace and, after spells working in Demark and Sweden, he joined the Nazi Party in 1923. He helped plan the Munich Beer Hall Putsch the same year, was wounded in the fighting, and fled to Austria, where he remained in exile until granted amnesty in 1926. He rejoined the party and won a seat in the Reichstag in 1928 and became its president in 1932. He became minister without portfolio and Prussia's minister of the interior in Hitler's first cabinet the following year. Further promotions followed—commander of the *Luftwaffe* in 1935 and minister of the economy in 1937. Two years later Hitler nominated Goering as his successor and elevated him to the rank of Reichsmarshall.

Goering's fame reached its peak from late 1939 to early 1940, largely because of the *Luftwaffe*'s excellent performance during the invasions of Poland and then of France and the Low Countries, but thereafter his prestige declined. The *Luftwaffe*'s failures at Dunkirk, when it was given the task of preventing the Anglo-French evacuation, and during the Battle of Britain, when it was supposed to destroy RAF Fighter Command prior to an invasion, marked the beginning of his fall. Matters worsened when British bombers started striking at targets in the Third Reich, a development that Goering had promised would never happen. His credibility was finally shattered by the debacle of the Stalingrad airlift in 1943; once again a proud boast that the *Luftwaffe* could supply the garrison alone was wildly wrong.

Goering lost influence to more ambitious Nazis in the final years of the war and, plagued by the morphine addiction he had contracted in the 1920s, he retreated to his vast estates. He was finally stripped of all his ranks and

Left: Goering discusses the progress of the Battle of Britain with one of his *Luftwaffe* pilots during the summer of 1940.

Left: *Luftwaffe* ground crew undertake a major service on a Messerschmitt Bf 110 twin-engined fighter during the campaign in North Africa.

Below: Goering is flanked by various senior figures in the *Luftwaffe*. From their demeanor, the picture was taken around the time of the fall of France.

positions by Hitler in 1945 after he had suggested that he should assume power if the latter was incapacitated in any way. Put on trial at Nuremburg, he escaped the noose by taking cyanide shortly before his planned execution.

Below: Goering discusses *Luftwaffe* matters with Udet. The latter gradually fell from favor not least because he was partly blamed for the Battle of Britain defeat.

Graziani, Rodolfo

(1882–1955) Nationality: Italian.
Senior position: Chief-of-Staff Italian Army.
Final rank: Marshal.

After stints as governor of Libya, viceroy of Ethiopia, and the Italian Army's chief-of-staff, Graziani was made commander-in-chief in North Africa in 1940. He mismanaged the invasion of Egypt and was removed in early 1941 but re-emerged briefly as Mussolini's minister of defense in 1943. Tried for treason in 1945, he served five years.

Above: A tired and disheveled Graziani pictured after being captured by the Allies in the latter stages of the war, when he was Mussolini's defense minister and chief-of-staff.

the position of chief of the general
staff in July 1944 but incurred Hitler's
wrath—Guderian invariably spoke his
mind—and was dismissed for a
second time in late March the following year.

Left: Guderian reads an intelligence report
that has just been decrypted by an Enigma
machine during the lightning drive by his XIX
Corps through France in May 1940.
Below: Guderian smiles for the camera
during the hectic race through northern
France.

Guderian, Heinz

(1888–1954) Nationality: German.
Senior position: Chief-of-Staff
  German Army.
Final rank: Colonel-General.

Guderian was a career army officer,
who in the late 1920s and 1930s
became a thoughtful advocate of
armored warfare. Although more
conservative officers rejected his
theories and suggestions, they found
favor with the Nazis after they came
to power in 1933. Guderian enjoyed
rapid promotion, becoming general of
armored troops in 1938. He held a
field command during the invasion of
Poland and was able to perfect the

idea of lightning war, or *Blitzkrieg*.
His forces achieved the decisive
breakthrough during the invasion of
France in May 1940 and he followed
this success on the Eastern Front
during the first month of the invasion
in 1941.

Guderian's luck ran out in
December as he was dismissed for
ordering a withdrawal. He remained
in retirement until March 1943, when
he was appointed inspector of
armored troops in the wake of the
Stalingrad defeat.. His main role was
to maintain the fighting efficiency of
the various armored divisions on the
Eastern Front and this he largely
achieved during 1943 and 1944,
despite the enormous difficulties.
Guderian was eventually promoted to

Halder, Franz
(1884–1975) Nationality: German.
Senior position: Chief of the General Staff.
Final rank: General.

Halsey, Willliam
(1882–1959) Nationality: American.
Senior position: Commander Third Fleet.
Final rank: Admiral.

Halder was made chief of the General Staff in 1938, despite his opposition to Hitler. He planned and oversaw the invasion of Poland and Western Europe, although he argued that the latter should be postponed. Halder served until 1942, when he was replaced and later imprisoned after being implicated in the Bomb Plot.

Halsey came from a naval family and graduated from Annapolis in 1904. He spent much of the interwar period serving on destroyers in various capacities, including being based at Queenstown, southern Ireland, during World War I. He also served as the US naval attaché in various European countries, including Germany, during

Above: Halder was a key figure in the first resistance movement against Hitler to form in the officer corps during 1938, but it came to nothing.

Above: Halsey strikes a suitably pugnacious pose. He had a well-earned reputation for toughness and earned the sobriquet "Bull."

the early 1920s and graduated from both the naval and army war colleges in the early 1930s. He completed flight training in 1935, and then began a long association with the navy's carrier force.

At the time of Pearl Harbor, he was

Below: Halsey (center) attends a meeting with various other US Navy officers, including Vice-Admiral John McCain (second from right), who died at sea in September 1945.

commander of Carrier Division 2. Over the first months of 1942 he conducted operations against Japanese-held islands in the Central Pacific and oversaw the Doolittle Raid on mainland Japan. After a period of illness Halsey was made commander of the South Pacific Area and in a series of battles in the southern Solomons had finally defeated the Japanese naval effort off Guadalcanal by November. Thereafter he directed

naval operations that liberated the rest of the Solomons in the second half of 1943, and then he moved on Bougainville, which fell the following year.

Halsey was given command of a fleet in June 1944 and took part in naval operations off Luzon in the Philippines, where his decision to send the greater part of his command to sink a number of Japanese carriers, thus leaving only a few warships to

cover the vital San Bernardino Strait, was criticized. Worse news followed when he unnecessarily sailed into a typhoon and lost three destroyers. Nevertheless Halsey, who was noted for his aggression and energy, recovered from these setbacks to sweep through the South China Sea in mid-January 1945 inflicting irreplaceable losses on the Japanese and, after a brief spell away from active service, he returned to take part in the Okinawa campaign during May and June. In the final months of the war he launched raids off the Japanese home islands. The official surrender ceremony was conducted on his flagship, USS *Missouri*, in Tokyo Bay on 2 September.

Below: Halsey, who liked to hit the enemy hard and fast, confers with another officer during a lull in the Pacific campaign.

Harris, Arthur

(1892–1984) Nationality: British.
Senior position: Commander RAF Bomber Command.
Final rank: Air Chief Marshal.

Harris served with a Rhodesian infantry regiment in Africa during the first years of World War I but then transferred to the Royal Flying Corps and took part in the air campaign over the Western Front for the remainder of the conflict. During the interwar years, he served as a pilot with the Royal Air Force's Home Defence Command and had long periods in both India and the Middle East. In the late 1930s he returned to England to serve on the staff but at the outbreak of war in 1939 Harris was in command of No. 5 Bomber Group.

He was soon promoted, serving as deputy chief of the Air Staff during 1940-1941 before becoming head of Bomber Command in February 1942. Harris, an absolute believer in air power, oversaw its rapid expansion and was completely sure that a major strategic bombing campaign against Germany's economic infrastructure would destroy its ability to wage war and thus force its surrender. He had, however, seen that precision bombing of individual targets in daylight had largely failed and resulted in heavy bomber losses, so from mid-1943 he turned to area bombing at night, effectively targeting large swathes of German cities. This was a controversial decision since it meant that German civilians would feel the brunt of his campaign.

Harris was popular with the men under his command but was something of a controversial figure, one often at odds with his colleagues. His strategic bombing campaign did serious damage to Germany's communications network but the raids did not significantly impair its industrial output. Nor did area bombing significantly undermine the morale of ordinary Germans as he had suggested it would. Equally, he only reluctantly agreed to use his bombers in support of the buildup to the Normandy

Right: "Bomber" Harris was much admired by those who served under him but his strategic bombing campaign against Germany remains a controversial topic.

landings in 1944, arguing that they should continue to strike targets inside Germany. Bomber Command also suffered very high losses during the campaign.

Harris retired in September 1945 and only belatedly received official recognition for his wartime role, becoming a baronet in 1953.

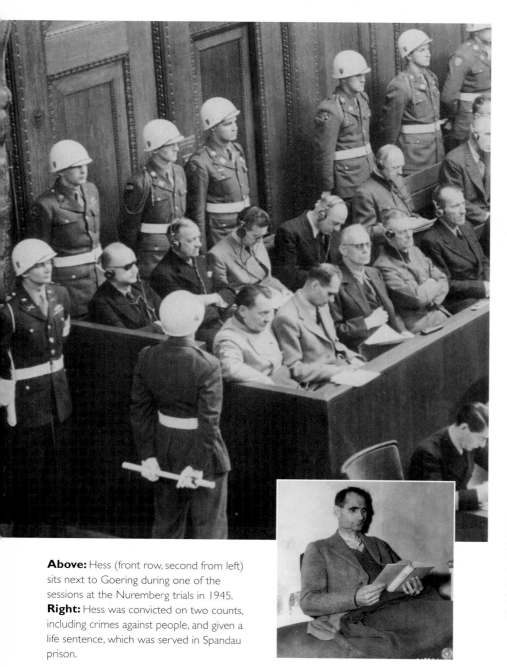

Hess, Rudolf

**(1896–1987) Nationality: German.
Senior position: Deputy Fuehrer.**

Hess was a longstanding supporter of and friend to Hitler—the two had served together in the same infantry regiment for a time during World War I before Hess transferred to the air arm. During the interwar years he fought with the right-wing *Freikorps*, studied at the University of Munich, and participated in the Nazis' unsuccessful Beer Hall Putsch in 1923. He was subsequently jailed and served his seven-month sentence with Hitler in Landsberg prison.

Hess became Hitler's personal secretary in 1925 and further promotions followed as he worked his way up the Nazi Party hierarchy. In 1933 he became Hitler's deputy, two years later he was permitted to have a say in the appointment of all senior Nazi officials, and in 1939 he was made a member of the key Ministerial Council for the Defense of the Reich. Hess astonished the wider world and infuriated Hitler, who dubbed him "insane," by flying to Britain in May 1941 on a mission the intent of which remains a matter of debate but was probably an attempt to secure peace. Hess was interrogated and imprisoned but was later tried at Nuremberg and given a life sentence. He hanged himself after spending forty-one years in Spandau prison.

Above: Hess (front row, second from left) sits next to Goering during one of the sessions at the Nuremberg trials in 1945.
Right: Hess was convicted on two counts, including crimes against people, and given a life sentence, which was served in Spandau prison.

Himmler, Heinrich

(1900–1945) Nationality: German.
Senior position: Reichsfuehrer of the SS.

Himmler was an early adherent to the Nazi cause, one who took part in the Beer Hall Putsch in Munich during 1923 and became head of the small SS, effectively the party's street-fighters, in 1929. He quickly turned the latter into a ruthlessly efficient organization that was used, with Hitler's backing, to smash the rival Brownshirts in the so-called "Blood Purge" of late June 1934. A year later Himmler was made head of the Third Reich's unified police system and he was put at the heart of the Nazis' racial polices in 1939, when he was made *Reich Commissar* for the Consolidation of German Nationhood, an organization that would devise and run the Final Solution.

Below: Members of the Waffen SS take part in one of the many parades that were so beloved by the Nazi hierarchy.

Heydrich, Reinhard

(1904–1942) Nationality: German.
Senior position: Deputy Reich Protector of Bohemia and Moravia.
Final rank: SS General.

Heydrich joined the SS in 1932 and, thanks to Himmler's support, enjoyed a meteoric rise. He was a dedicated Nazi and attended the Wannsee Conference of January 1942, where he was given the job of implementing the Final Solution. He was ambushed in Prague in late May by Czech resistance fighters and died from his wounds.

Above: It is believed that Heydrich was being considered as Hitler's successor.

As the war progressed Hitler came to depend more and more on Himmler and the vastly expanded SS, which he saw as the embodiment of Nazism, and especially so after the 1944 Bomb Plot, which was largely carried out by army officers. In early 1945 Himmler was put in charge of the *Volksturm* militia units tasked with defending Berlin. However, previously loyal, Himmler was soon making clumsy attempts to secure a separate peace with the western Allies. Hitler ordered his arrest but he actually fell into Allied hands, and was able to commit suicide by taking cyanide.

Below: Himmler held a number of positions during the war but derived much of his power from his leadership of the SS.

Above: Hitler and various other members of the Nazi leadership gave speeches at Berlin's Kroll Opera House, probably in May 1941.

Hirohito

**(1901–1989) Nationality: Japanese.
Senior position: Emperor.**

Hirohito, who was seen as a living god by those he reigned over, ascended the imperial throne in 1926 but his powers were actually rather limited. He was present at cabinet meetings but tradition dictated that he could not participate in any discussions and could do no more than give his ascent to any decisions taken. Indeed, the system was so hidebound that ministers never asked him to give an opinion on any matter for fear of causing embarrassment. Yet, for all this, any decisions, orders or proclamations made in public bore his name, including the one declaring war on the United States.

In reality Hirohito had made some efforts to slow the rush to war and, as the situation deteriorated, he became somewhat bolder, at one point sending a peace mission to the Soviet Union. The emperor finally expressed his views to a deadlocked cabinet in early August 1945, declaring that he was willing to accept surrender terms, even though they might endanger his own position. He announced the surrender to his people on the 15 August, but the Allies allowed him to keep his throne by the Allies, although he had to relinquish his divinity in January 1946.

Right: The Japanese emperor pictured dressed in traditional costume.

Hitler, Adolf

(1889–1945) Nationality: Naturalized German.
Senior position: Fuehrer and Chancellor of the Third
Reich.

Hitler had an undistinguished, unhappy childhood and youth but rushed to join the colors when World War I broke out in 1914. He served with distinction, being wounded and receiving the Iron Cross, but never rose above the rank of corporal. His interest in politics came after 1918, when he came to believe that impoverished Germany had been

Above: In a photograph taken shortly after the July Bomb Plot, Hitler is surrounded by several leading Nazis including a clearly wounded Jodl.

betrayed by those who had sought peace—in his mind chiefly socialists and Jews—and that men like him had a mission to recapture its former glory. He was drawn to extremist right wing politics and took over the fledgling National Socialist German Workers' Party, or Nazi Party, in the early 1920s and set about turning it into an effective political force. Hitler attempted to seize power through an armed uprising, the Beer Hall Putsch in Munich during November 1923. It was a fiasco and he was sent to prison, where he spent his time writing the rambling and deeply anti-Semitic book *Mein Kampf* (My Struggle) that, among other things, also attempted to explain his political views and outline solutions to Germany's woes.

Hitler vowed to win power through the ballot box, although he continued to use street violence against those he saw as his opponents, chiefly members of socialist organizations and trade unions. He eventually won power in 1933, becoming chancellor, and set about consolidating his powers, not hesitating to deal ruthlessly with members of his own party if he suspected them of disloyalty or saw them as rivals. Within eighteen months of becoming chancellor, he been given dictatorial powers and had been named presi-

Below: Various top Nazis and other party members salute Hitler in the Kroll Opera House, home to the German parliament after the 1933 Reichstag fire.

dent, and the persecution of the Jewish community, which would lead to some six million deaths in concentration and extermination camps, had been speeded up. He also abolished the democratic process and set about creating an all-encompassing Nazi state. He also pushed forward a major rearmament program in contravention of the 1914–1918 peace settlements and began to flex his muscles on the international stage, sensing that other leading European powers would do little to intervene. In 1936 he reoccupied the demilitarized

Rhineland and two years later began to expand Germany's borders. Austria was annexed first, with the Sudetenland in Czechoslovakia the following year. The remainder was gobbled up in 1939.

Hitler now sought to make Germany the dominant power in Europe. His invasion of Poland in 1939 provoked Britain and France to declare war but the latter was defeated by June 1940 and the former left isolated for twelve months or so. Hitler's invasion plan for Britain was thwarted by the latter's victory in the

Battle of Britain, but by the end of the year he was increasingly focused on waging a racial and ideological war against the Soviet Union. This began in June 1941 and the invasion, Operation Barbarossa, was a turning point. The Red Army buckled but did not collapse, and effectively gained the initiative on the Eastern Front from late 1942, with the Russian counterattacks around Stalingrad. By this stage Hitler was also at war with the United States and the Third Reich was slowly crumbling, not least because its economy was not geared up to fight a prolonged war.

Hitler had also turned on his own armed forces, especially the army, which he suspected of disloyalty. He had made himself supreme commander in late 1941, despite having no appropriate experience, and became more and more antagonistic to his commanders as the military situation deteriorated further. Germany was in an increasingly parlous state by the end of 1943—defeat on the Eastern Front was all but inevitable, Italy had surrendered, German cities were being increasingly pulverized by Allied bombers, the Battle of the Atlantic had turned decisively in the Allies' favor, and an invasion of Western Europe was imminent—yet Hitler determined to fight on. This prompted an attempt on his life in July 1944, shortly after the Allied landings in Normandy plunged Germany

Below: Various generals attend Hitler during a meeting to discuss strategy. One of them, Stauffenberg (second from left) would be a key figure in the July Bomb Plot.

into a war on two fronts.

Defeat became inevitable with the failure of the Ardennes offensive in late 1944 to early 1945, but Hitler, who was increasingly detached from reality partly through the drugs he was taking and partly through nervous exhaustion, retreated to his underground bunker in central Berlin. Here he spent his final days, living in something approaching a fantasy world that bore no relation to events on the outside. Hitler was surrounded by a small band of his most loyal acolytes, including Bormann and Goebbels, but many other senior Nazis, including Goering and Himmler, sought to save their own skins.

The final act began on 29 August when Hitler married his long-standing mistress Eva Braun and also penned both his personal political testament and will. The next day the newly-weds retired to his suite and Hitler shot himself. Braun took poison and both bodies were then hurriedly cremated in a shallow hole outside the bunker, even as Russian artillery fire rained down from nearby.

Hitler's legacy was not the "1,000 Year Reich"—it had lasted a mere twelve or so—but suffering on an unparalleled scale, not least among the German people whom he ultimately blamed for his defeat, that stretched not only across Europe but also ran far beyond its borders.

Right: Hitler, seen here with Speer (left), paid just one visit to Paris during the war, shortly after the fall of France in 1940.

Hodges, Courtney

(1887–1966) Nationality: American.
Senior position: Commander First
  Army.
Final rank: General.

Hodges dropped out of West Point in 1905 and enlisted in the US Army as a private, where he rose through the ranks during service in Mexico and on the Western Front during World War I. In the interwar years he served in various staff positions and attended the Army War College. Between 1938 and 1940 he served at the Infantry School, first as its deputy commandant and from October 1940 as its commandant. Thereafter he was named as the chief of infantry until the post was abolished in early 1942, whereupon he was tasked with establishing the Training and School Command.

After various other home commands Hodges traveled to Europe in early 1944 and commanded a US army during the breakout from the Normandy beaches. His troops liberated Paris, participated in the bitter battle for the Huertgen Forest, and bore the brunt of the fighting during the Battle of the Bulge at the year's end. Thereafter, they secured the Ludendorff Bridge over the River Rhine at Remagen in March 1945 and drove deep into Germany until Hodges' advanced units linked up with the Red Army at Torgau on the River Elbe on 25 April, just days before the end of the war.

Above Hodges made three-star lieutenant-general in February 1943.

Horrocks, Brian

(1895–1985) Nationality: British.
Senior position: Commander XXX Corps.
Final rank: Lieutenant-General.

Montgomery thought Horrocks his best corps commander, and the two served together in France in 1940, North Africa, and in Sicily, where Horrocks was severely wounded. He returned to action in August 1944 to participate in the Normandy breakout, the liberation of Belgium, the Arnhem operation, and the final push into Germany.

Left: Horrocks, commander of Britain's XXX Corps, at the wheel of a staff car during the race through France in the second half of 1944.

Horton, Max

(1883–1951) Nationality: British.
Senior position: Commander-in-Chief Western Approaches.
Final rank: Admiral.

Horton held several senior posts during the war years. In 1942 he was tasked with protecting the Atlantic convoys that were being menaced by some 400 U-boats. Although the situation was perilous, he was able to effectively defeat the submarines by May 1943, winning arguably the most important campaign of the war.

Left: Horton (second from left) was a brilliant naval strategist, overseeing the defeat of the German U-boat flotillas.

Hoth, Herrmann

(1885–1971) Nationality: German
Senior position: Commander Fourth Panzer Army
Final rank: General

Hoth was an excellent commander of armoured forces and took part in some major victories during the invasion of Russia in 1941. He then fought in the Battle for Stalingrad, where his panzer army narrowly failed to relieve the encircled German garrison.. He next served at Kursk but was sacked by Hitler in late 1943.

Above: A German Mark III tank fords a wide but shallow river somewhere in Russia during the summer of 1941.
Left: Hoth, who commanded the Third Panzer Army during the opening phase of Operation Barbarossa, stands to attention as troops parade past him.

Above: Hoth stands trial at Nuremberg on war crimes charges. Sentenced to fifteen years in 1948, he was released after just six.

Hull, Cordell

(1871–1955) Nationality: American.
Senior position: Secretary of State.

Responsible for foreign relations before and during the Japanese attack on Pearl Harbor, Cordell Hull, the longest-serving secretary of state (eleven years, 1933–1944), was receiving the Japanese ambassador and special envoy to discuss the "Outline of Proposed Basis for Agreement Between The United States and Japan." The attack had just taken place, and Hull glanced at their copy of the fourteen-part message (Japan's declaration that negotiations were at an end) and could not contain himself. "In all my fifty years of public service," he told the diplomats, "I have never seen such a document that was more crowded with infamous falsehood and distortion."

Hull's legacy, though, was the drafting of the "Charter of the United Nations," even as the fighting in the Pacific and in Europe was increasing in ferocity, For such work he received the Nobel Peace Prize in 1945.

Above: Hull did not enjoy the best of help during the war, but proved a fairly effective secretary of state.

Hyakutake, Haruyoshi

**(1888–1947) Nationality: Japanese.
Senior position: Commander
   Seventeenth Army.
Final rank: Lieutenant-General.**

After holding various staff and command positions at home, Hyakutake took charge of an army to consolidate Japanese gains in the southwest Pacific. He failed in this and his army was ground down by fighting in the Solomons between mid-1942 and mid-1944. After attachment to the Eighth Army, he returned home in 1946.

Below: Hyakutake commanded Japanese troops based in the Solomons but was unable to prevent the US capture of Guadalcanal.

Imamura, Hitoshi

**(1886–1968) Nationality: Japanese.
Senior position: Commander
   Sixteenth/Eighteenth Armies.
Final rank: General.**

Above: Imamura was widely regarded as one of Japan's best generals and took commanded of two armies in the Southwest Pacific in 1943.

Previously vice-chief-of-staff to the Kwantung Army in China, Imamura was given an army to take Java in the Dutch East Indies in 1942. He was stationed on Rabaul from 1943 and successfully dislocated the movement of supplies to US troops on Guadalcanal. Later convicted of war crimes, he was released in 1954.

Ironside, Edmund
(1880–1959) Nationality: British.
Senior position: Chief of the Imperial General Staff.
Final rank: Field Marshal.

Ismay, Hastings
(1887–1965) Nationality: British.
Senior position: Churchill's chief-of-staff.
Final rank: General.

Ironside was inspector general of Overseas Forces in 1939 and, although he wished to take command of the British Expeditionary Force, he was actually made chief of the Imperial General Staff. He held this post until May 1940 when he became commander-in-chief Home Forces.

Above: Ironside's tenure as chief of the Imperial General Staff was overshadowed by the British Army's poor showing in the early part of the war.

Hastings became head of the Secretariat of the Committee of Imperial Defence in 1939 but in 1940 he was made Churchill's personal chief-of-staff, a conduit for the flow of information between the prime minister and various other senior figures, especially in the military. He also liaised with their US counterparts and proved outstandingly effective.

Above: Ismay (standing behind Churchill) was a "desk" general but proved a calming influence on his political superior.

Jodl, Alfred

(1890–1946) Nationality: German.
Senior position: Chief-of-Staff
    Operations Staff.
Final rank: Colonel-General.

Jodl, a brilliant if over-ambitious careerist soldier who regarded Hitler as Germany's savior, was in 1938 deputy head of the Operations Staff of the *Oberkommando der Wehrmacht*, effectively the high command of the German armed forces, and became its head a year later. He proved a loyal servant to Hitler throughout the war and effectively directed operations on most fronts. The two had several major disagreements over strategic policy and Jodl's influence waned in the latter stages of the conflict.

Jodl did request a field command in 1942 after the dismissal of two senior officers but was refused. He was injured during the Bomb Plot in July 1944, and signed the German Army's unconditional surrender document at Reims on 7 May 1945. He was tried at Nuremberg as a "planner of aggressive war" and, despite arguing that his actions were dictated by a "soldier's obedience," was found guilty on four counts, including crimes against humanity, and hanged.

Right: Although by no means an out-and-out supporter of National Socialism, Jodl had been involved in right-wing politics during the 1930s and was a great admirer of Hitler.

Above: Jodl signs the unconditional surrender documents as drawn up by the Allies on 7 May 1945 on behalf of Doenitz's short-lived government. It came into effect at 2301 hours the following day.

Right: Jodl (top right) waits to sign the unconditional surrender documents at Eisenhower's headquarters.

Joubert de la Ferte, Philip

(1896–1965) Nationality: British.
Senior position: Commander-in-Chief RAF Coastal
  Command.
Final rank: Air Chief Marshal.

Philip Joubert de la Ferte was in charge of the RAF's Coastal Command from 1941 until 1943 and made several tactical and technological innovations that eventually did much to help combat the U-boat menace. He was appointed to the staff of Lord Mountbatten's Southeast Asia Command in 1943.

Juin, Alphonse

(1888–1967) Nationality: French.
Senior position: Commander French Expeditionary
  Force.
Final Rank: General.

Juin was captured by the Germans in1940 but released thanks to the intercession of the Vichy authorities, but he refused the latters' offer of the post of war minister. He became the commander of their forces in North Africa but joined the Allies and led the French Expeditionary Corps in Italy in 1943. He then served in Western Europe.

Kai-shek, Chiang

(1887–1975) Nationality: Chinese.
Senior position: Nationalist leader.
Final rank: Generalissimo.

Although initially destined for the civil service, Chiang Kai-shek opted for a career in the military and studied at colleges in both China and Japan. He became embroiled in a number of uprisings against China's corrupt warlords

Above: Chiang Kai-shek addresses a gathering of his Nationalist supporters before the outbreak of World War II.

who ruled much of the country in the second decade of the twentieth century, spent some time in exile, and in 1923 joined the Kuomintang, the Nationalist Party, which was dedicated to re-establishing central authority. His anti-corruption campaigns in the 1920s were only partly successful and Chiang increasingly turned to suppressing China's growing communist movement.

In 1935 Chiang was named chairman of the Kuomintang's Executive Council, a position that made him the effective ruler of China. Japan began to menace the country and in 1936 he reached an uneasy agreement with the communists to present a united front against a common enemy. The Japanese did invade the following year and Chiang was unable to prevent them from overrunning a sizeable part of the country. He retreated, establishing his capital in Chungking (Chongqing), while the communists remained behind in the occupied lands to wage a guerrilla campaign of varying intensity and success.

After Pearl Harbor in December 1941, Chiang began to receive US aid (never enough in his opinion) and advisers and, at the latter's behest, sent armies to fight on other fronts, most notably in Burma. The generalissimo was a demanding ally and he had frequent disagreements with Stilwell, his main US adviser, which did little to aid the Allied cause. Chiang did indeed get increased aid through Lend-Lease but much of it went not to fighting the Japanese but to the eradication of his likely postwar rivals—the communists.

He also demanded that US long-range bombers be sited on Chinese soil but this only provoked a major and mostly successful Japanese offensive. The US Joint Chiefs-of-Staff wanted the experienced Stilwell made commander-in-chief of Chinese forces, but Chiang's response was to demand the former's dismissal. Although he was recognized as China's legitimate ruler by the Allies at the war's end, his power was on the wane and he was forced into exile by the communists after a bitter civil war.

Below: Chiang Kai-shek attends a meeting in Cairo with Roosevelt and Churchill during November 1943.

Keitel, Wilhelm

(1882–1946) Nationality: German.
Senior position: Head of OKW.
Final rank: Field Marshal.

Keitel, a careerist soldier, really came to prominence in 1938 when the War Ministry and army high command, previously separate organizations, were united on Hitler's orders to form the *Oberkommando der Wehrmacht*, effectively a unified high command governing all three branches of the armed forces. Keitel was made its head and soon earned a reputation among his peers as an arch sycophant, one always eager to carry out Hitler's orders without question or hesitation. He even claimed that Hitler was the greatest soldier of all time and became so disliked by some that he became known to his detractors as *Lakaitel*, a play on the German word for lackey—*Lakai*.

Although he was present at meetings to discuss military strategy and related matters, he rarely proffered an opinion unless asked to comment directly by Hitler, and any statements he made usually took the form of largely uncontroversial advice. In reality much of the OKW's day-to-day business was conducted by far more able deputies, including Jodl. Keitel remained absolutely loyal to Hitler to the end but argued that he was only obeying orders when put on trial at Nuremberg. He was found guilty of war crimes and crimes against humanity, however, and hanged.

Below: Keitel signs the ratification document that confirms Germany's unconditional surrender in Berlin, 9 May 1945.

Kesselring, Albrecht

(1885–1960) Nationality: German.
Senior position: Commander-in-
Chief South.
Final rank: Field Marshal.

Above: Kesselring, nicknamed "Smiling Albert," pays a visit to North Africa during his time as the *Luftwaffe*'s commander-in-chief south.

Right: Although he trained as an air officer, Kesselring proved a first-rate commander of ground troops during the Italian campaign.

Kesselring embarked on a military career as an artillery officer but transferred to the emerging *Luftwaffe* in 1933. Holding senior rank by the

outbreak of the war in 1939, he commanded air fleets during the invasions of Poland and France and the Low Countries and directed

Luftflotte II from bases in northeast France and Belgium during the Battle of Britain in 1940. His fighters came close to dealing RAF Fighter Command a mortal blow but Goering's change of strategy to bombing London severely restricted his freedom of operation. Heavy losses among Kesselring's bomber crews effectively led to defeat.

Kesselring was then dispatched to Italy as commander-in-chief during 1941 and, although based in Rome, he was closely involved in the North African campaign, but despaired at the lack of aircraft to keep the German forces fighting there supplied. His fortunes improved when the Allies invaded Sicily and the Italian mainland during 1943 and Kesselring proved to be a very able commander of ground troops fighting largely defensive battles. He became commander-in-chief west in March 1945 but could do little more than negotiate a surrender with the Americans. Tried for war crimes in Italy, his death sentence was commuted to life imprisonment but he was released on health grounds in 1952.

Below: Kesselring prepares to board a Junkers Ju 52 transport aircraft for a trip to North Africa.

King, Ernst

(1878–1974) Nationality: American.
Senior position: Chief of Naval
Operations.
Final rank: Admiral.

King, a dominant figure in US naval affairs, held the position of chief of naval operations from early 1942 and also served on the US Joint Chiefs-of-Staff and the Anglo-American Combined Chiefs-of-Staff. He left operational command to officers like Nimitz, but he helped to design the island-hopping strategy that achieved victory in the Pacific.

Above: King was a brilliant naval strategist but not always easy to get along with.

Kinkaid, Thomas

(1888–1972) Nationality: American.
Senior position: Commander 7th
   Fleet.
Final rank: Admiral.

Kleist, Paul von

(1881–1954) Nationality: German.
Senior position: Commander Army
   Group A.
Final rank: Field Marshal.

Kinkaid made his reputation as an aggressive commander in battles off Guadalcanal, first with aircraft carriers and then a cruiser squadron. He then briefly served in the Aleutians campaign before being given command of a fleet, a mix of transports and carriers that took part in the Battle of Leyte Gulf in the Philippines during late 1944.

Above: Kinkaid played a distinguished role in the Battle of Leyte Gulf in October 1944.

Kleist was an expert in armored warfare and served with distinction on the Western and Eastern Fronts. He led the First Panzer Group in 1941 and captured some 660,000 Soviet troops. He took the First Panzer Army into the Caucasus in 1942, only narrowly avoiding encirclement himself. He was captured while commanding an army group in 1944.

Above: Germany artillery crosses a French river, May 1940.

Above: A formal portrait of Kleist.

Kluge, Gunther von

(1882–1944) Nationality: German.
Senior position: Commander-in-Chief West.
Final rank: Field Marshal.

Koga, Mineichi

(1885–1944) Nationality: Japanese.
Senior position: Commander Combined Fleet.
Final rank: Admiral.

An army commander during the *Blitzkriegs* on Poland, and France and the Low Countries during 1939-1940, Kluge was later commander of an army group on the Eastern Front. Transferred west in mid-1944, he failed to halt the Allied breakout from Normandy and, under suspicion, was recalled to Berlin but took poison during the journey.

Koga was a career naval officer who took over the Combined Fleet, the Imperial Japanese Navy's main strike force, after the death of his predecessor, Yamamoto, in April 1943. Koga sought but never achieved a decisive victory over the US Pacific Fleet and he was killed when his aircraft crashed during a tropical storm.

Above: Kluge, from an aristocratic background, was part of a failed prewar plot to have Hitler replaced.

Above: Koga, an expert in naval surface warfare but who underestimated the importance of carrier-based aircraft.

Kondo, Nobutake

(1886–1953) Nationality: Japanese.
Senior position: Commander 2nd Fleet.
Final rank: Admiral.

Konev, Ivan

(1897–1973) Nationality: Russian.
Senior position: Commander 1st Ukrainian Front.
Final rank: Marshal.

Kondo was commander of the 2nd Fleet in 1941 and directed operations that led to the sinking of the Royal Navy's *Prince of Wales* and *Repulse* on 10 December. In 1942 he led the Support Force at the Battles of Midway and then fought in the southwest Pacific. He was present at the Battles of the Eastern Solomons, Santa Cruz, and Guadalcanal.

Above: A gunnery expert and a capable staff officer, Kondo lacked the drive to be a fighting admiral of stature.

Konev was an extremely competent commander who served in various senior posts on the Eastern Front. He first commanded a front (group) of armies from late 1941 and helped stop the German offensive at Kursk in 1943. Thereafter he commanded the 2nd and 1st Ukranian Fronts, fighting his way to the River Elbe with the latter in May 1945.

Above: Konev was an able commander but always in Zhukov's shadow, having been beaten by him to several senior posts.

Krueger, Walter

(1881–1967) Nationality: American.
Senior position: Commander Sixth Army.
Final rank: Lieutenant-General.

Kurita, Takeo

(1889–1977) Nationality: Japanese.
Senior position: Commander Strike Force One.
Final rank: Admiral.

Krueger, who was a very able general, took charge of the Sixth Army in early 1943 and served throughout the war under MacArthur in the Southwest Pacific. His troops fought in numerous battles, including the campaigns in New Guinea and New Britain, before embarking on the liberation of the Philippines in late 1944.

Above: Krueger was an able ground commander in the Pacific campaign but, unlike MacArthur, publicity-shy.

Kurita took part in the Battle of Midway in 1942, where he led the Japanese navy's Close Support Force but in late 1944 he was commanding the powerful Strike Force One during the Battle of Leyte Gulf. His strike force sank a considerable number of US warships but he was forced to withdraw after two hours without achieving a decisive victory.

Above: Kurita, a sea-going admiral, spent the greater part of the war in various offensive and defensive operations.

Leahy, William

(1875–1959) Nationality: American.
Senior position: Roosevelt's Chief-
of-Staff.
Final rank: Admiral.

Leahy's role was never clearly defined but he was effectively the president's representative to the US Joint Chiefs-of-Staff and was a conduit for the flow of information between the two. He held almost daily meetings with Roosevelt and served in a similar capacity under his successor Truman.

Left: Leahy, a friend of Roosevelt during World War I, served in various posts during the conflict with Japan.

Leclerc, Philippe

(1902–1957) Nationality: French.
Senior position: Commander 2nd
Armored Division.
Final rank: General.

Leclerc was captured in 1940 and escaped twice, finally reaching England. He joined the Free French cause and served as governor of Chad and Cameroon and as commander of forces in Equatorial Africa. He then led a Free French force fighting in North Africa and ended the war commanding an armored unit in Western Europe.

Above: Leclerc's real name was Viscount Philippe de Hauteclocque. Here he directs operations of the French 2nd Armored Division.

Leeb, Wilhelm von

(1876–1956) Nationality: German.
Senior position: Commander Army
  Group North.
Final rank: Field Marshal.

Leeb actually retired from the army in 1938 but was recalled the following year and given command of Army Group C for the invasion of Poland, and in 1940 he led it during the invasion of France and the Low Countries. He was placed in charge of Army Group North for the invasion of the Soviet Union, but was sacked in January 1942.

Left: Hitler described the aristocratic Leeb as an "incorrigible anti-Nazi," yet often called on his skills.

Leese, Oliver

(1894–1978) Nationality: British.
Senior position: Commander Allied
  Land Forces Southeast Asia.
Final rank: General.

Leese led a corps in the Eightt Army and served in North Africa and Sicily before replacing Montgomery as its commander in January 1944 at the height of the Italian campaign. He served in the position with some success until the following November and was then transferred to the Far East.

Below: Leese (left, with Sir Henry Maitland Wilson) received a knighthood in the field.

Leigh-Mallory, Trafford

(1892–1944) Nationality: British.
Senior position: Commander-in-Chief Allied Air Forces.
Final rank: Air Marshal.

Leigh-Mallory commanded the RAF's No. 12 Fighter Group when the war began in 1939 and he led these squadrons during the Battle of Britain, where they flew in defense of southeast England from the bases in the south Midlands. He advocated the use of the so-called Big Wing, which consisted of several fighter squadrons, to intercept the *Luftwaffe*'s raiders, but some of his colleagues felt such formations took too long to form up at altitude. There were bitter arguments, but he survived the controversy to become commander of No. 11 Fighter Group in December 1940 and head of Fighter Command itself in late 1942.

The next year Leigh-Mallory was made commander-in-chief of Allied air forces for the Normandy landings and again became embroiled in controversy when he attempted to gain personal control of the Allied strategic bombing force for the buildup to the operation. Nevertheless, his proposal to bomb German lines of communications was accepted and proved highly successful. He was next posted to the Far East but died in an air crash while en route.

Above: Leigh-Mallory was often in conflict with his fellow officers over air tactics.

LeMay, Curtis

(1906–1990) Nationality: American.
Senior position: Commander
Twentieth Air Force.
Final rank: General.

LeMay gained his pilot's wings in 1929 and began his career flying fighters before transferring at his own request to the 305th Bombardment Group in 1937. He took part in tests to demonstrate the feasibility of bombers attacking ships at sea, was one of the first pilots to fly the B-17 Flying Fortress, and was given command of a bomber squadron in the 34th Bombardment Group. After a series of rapid promotions, he took over the 305th in April 1942 and took it to eastern England, where the US Eighth Army Air Force was being formed for precision strategic bombing raids on Germany in daylight.

LeMay set about trying to improve the force's largely lamentable bombing accuracy by stopping evasive maneuvers over targets and improving pre-mission briefings. He was rewarded with command of the 3rd Bombardment Division in June 1943 and led it during the Regensburg mission in August. LeMay then transferred to China in August 1944 to take charge of the 20th Bomber Command, which was conducting strategic bombing operations against mainland Japan. He then moved to the recently captured island of Guam to take charge of the 21st Bomber Group in January 1945 and set about improving

its success rate.

LeMay increased the payloads of the B-29 Superfortresses under his command by removing any unneces-

Above: LeMay was a key figure in organizing the daylight strategic bombing campaigns against both Germany and Japan.

sary weight, including machine guns and their gunners as the Japanese fighter forces was dwindling away to nothing, and ordered low-level attacks using a mix of incendiaries and high-explosive bombs but with an increasing emphasis on the former. He recognized that much of Japan's industrial base was not found in large factories but in small, often widely dispersed buildings, so precision bombing was not practical and only area bombing would work.

The new method proved devastatingly successful—B-29 losses also fell noticeably—and most of Japan's major (and largely wood-built) cities went up in flames over the following months, although a shortage of incendiaries caused a brief halt to the campaign. In July, LeMay's reward was to be given command of the two bombing units, which were designated the Twentieth Air Force.

Above: A pair of B-29 Superfortresses, the long-range bomber that laid waste large swathes of Japan's towns and cities.
Left: LeMay (right) pictured with Stilwell during the former's time in the China-Burma-Indian theater.

MacArthur, Douglas

(1880–1964) Nationality: American.
Senior position: Command-in-Chief
US Pacific Ground Forces.
Final rank: General of the Army.

MacArthur graduated from West Point in 1903 and over the next few years held positions in the Philippines, took various staff posts, and won the Medal of Honor during the Vera Cruz expedition in 1914. Following US entry into World War I, he helped raise the 42nd Division and then served first as its chief-of-staff and then commander in France. MacArthur served as superintendent of West Point and was the US Army's chief-of-staff, but he spent the greater part of the interwar period in the Philippines, which he helped to prepare for independence from the United States in 1935. His work remained incomplete so he resigned from the army in 1937 rather than be ordered home so that he could continue his work for the Filipino government.

As war with Japan became more likely, he returned to active duty and was named commander of US Army forces in the Far East in July 1941. He rapidly raised the islands' defense

Left: MacArthur, pictured here with his signature corncob pipe, was a supreme self-publicist and expert manipulator of the media.
Right: MacArthur stands on the bridge of his command vessel during an amphibious operation.

force from a mere 22,000 men to 180,000 but most of the new Filipino recruits had received little training before war broke out and quickly deserted. His garrison was caught out by Japanese air attacks on the local air bases on 8 December but he recovered to organize a well-planned fighting retreat down Luzon's Bataan Peninsula once the main Japanese invasion had begun.

As the situation in the Philippines became wholly untenable, he was ordered to Australia by the president and left on 11 March 1942, but vowed to return to liberate the country. He was named the supreme commander of all the Allied forces in what was designated the Southwest Pacific Area. However, MacArthur was somewhat hamstrung in that he

actually commanded just 25,000 troops and around 250 mostly obsolete aircraft. His demands for extra men and equipment were later met in part but, because the Allies had a "Germany first" agreement and other commitments in the Pacific, he was never entirely satisfied and frequently made his views known to his superiors in the strongest possible terms.

Despite these ongoing shortages, his first operation was to secure Papua New Guinea, a potential springboard for an attack on Australia, by first throwing back a Japanese drive directed against Port Moresby on its south coast and then pushing across the tortuous Owen Stanley Range to take various key towns on the island's north coast. The

mission, which opened in July, was largely accomplished by late January 1943, although MacArthur frequently complained to his field commanders about the slow pace of their advance.

MacArthur was now able to launch his own counter-offensive through the Southwest Pacific, with the Philippines as the ultimate prize. Over the next several months he initi-

Below: MacArthur fulfills his promise to return to the Philippines, wading ashore in a highly dramatic scene on 20 October 1944.

ated a leap-frogging amphibious advance along Papua New Guinea's north coast but always insuring that the landings enjoyed a protective umbrella of land-based aircraft. It was a simple but highly effective strategy that reflected and was partly dictated by his lack of naval air power, most of which was serving in the Central Pacific where the islands needing recapture were much farther apart. His forces also took the island of New Britain during December and victory there insured that the main Japanese

base in the region, Rabaul, was effectively cut off from outside help and could mostly "wither on the vine."

By mid-1944, after landings on Hollandia and Aitape had cut off the Japanese Eighteenth Army by April, MacArthur's drive through the Southwest Pacific Area had almost converged with the similar thrust though the Central Pacific Area and the two forces could begin laying plans for the capture of the Philippines. The first troops landed on Leyte in October and further forces

landed on Luzon, the main island, in January 1945. MacArthur's units faced a determined enemy garrison that often fought to the bitter end, no more so than in the capital, Manila, which was virtually leveled before it was finally taken. Nevertheless, the various islands were gradually secured between February and August.

Even as the fighting in the Philippines raged, MacArthur turned to other targets, including the valuable coastal oilfields in Borneo, which were also largely secured by August. He was also given charge of all US ground forces in the theater during April, as a prelude to the final

Above: MacArthur adds his signature to the Japanese unconditional surrender document.

invasion of the Japanese home islands, but these amphibious assaults never took place due to the dropping of the atomic bombs on Hiroshima and Nagasaki. MacArthur's final act of the war was to accept the Japanese surrender on the battleship USS *Missouri* in Tokyo Bay on 2 September. He was subsequently commander of the occupation forces in Japan.

Mannerheim, Carl von

(1867–1951) Nationality: Finnish.
Senior position: Head of State.
Final rank: Marshal.

Manstein, Erich von

(1898–1967) Nationality: German.
Senior position: Commander Army Group South.
Final position: Field Marshal.

Mannerheim was a careerist officer who had fought in World War I and was recalled to defeat the Soviet invasion of his homeland in 1939. He narrowly failed but did secure favorable peace terms. He resumed hostilities in 1941 following Hitler's invasion of his former foe, but was again able to secure excellent armistice terms from the Russians in 1944.

Above: Mannerheim was an excellent soldier but he was an equally adept politician and diplomat.

Manstein was a career soldier who had been severely wounded in World War I but continued to serve in the postwar, much-reduced German Army. He is widely acknowledged as Hitler's finest general, his reputation largely resting on his twin abilities to plan complex offensives and undertake difficult missions against more numerous opponents. Manstein came to the fore in 1940 when, as chief-of-staff to the commander of Army Group A, he proposed an alternative plan for the

Left: Somewhere on the Eastern Front, Manstein (left) confers with a fellow officer.
Below: Manstein was a capable commander, his greatest exploit being the recapture of Kharkov in February 1943.

invasion of France and the Low Countries that was largely accepted by his superiors.

Manstein's strategy proved highly successful and he was given command of an armored corps and then the Eleventh Army during the first stages of the invasion of the Soviet Union. He took over an army group in mid-1942 and, in his first fireman's role, came close to relieving Stalingrad in December. His greatest

victory against the odds came in 1943 when he recaptured Kharkov, but he gradually incurred Hitler's wrath after failure at the Battle of Kursk. Manstein preferred to maneuver his forces to gain advantage rather than simply hold ground of no military value, but Hitler saw this tactic as a cover for unauthorized retreats. He turned against the field marshal and dismissed him in early 1944.

Mao Zhe-dong

**(1893–1976) Nationality: Chinese.
Senior position: Chairman Chinese
Communist Party.**

Mao was a close ally of Stalin until the late 1920s, when directives issued by the Comintern led to a wave of violence against Chinese communists by the opposing Nationalists of the Kuomintang. Despite their rivalries and animosities the latter two groupings made an uneasy alliance in the face of Japanese aggression, although in reality both continued their undeclared ideological conflict even as they battled the invaders. Mao remained behind in areas occupied by the Japanese and began to win the hearts and minds of the locals while launching a rural-based guerrilla campaign against the enemy.

The pact between Mao and the Nationalists gradually fell apart but was effectively over by 1940, by which stage Mao was expanding his operations against the latter from his power base at Yenan in Shanxi Province,

Above: Mao (center) photographed with his close colleague Chou En-Lai and Patrick Hurley, the US ambassador to China in 1943.

which he had reached after the famous Long March in 1935. The United States tried to renegotiate a new understanding between the two in 1944, but failed. When Japan surrendered in 1945 Mao controlled much of northern China and was poised to embark on the civil war that would bring him to power four years later.

Marshall, George

**(1880–1959) Nationality: American.
Senior position: Chief-of-Staff US
  Army.
Final rank: General of the Army.**

Marshall served as a junior officer on the staff of the commander-in-chief of the American Expeditionary Force during World War I, and then returned home to take various staff and other appointments. He undertook his first major planning role when he was made head of the War Plan's Division of the Army General Staff and then deputy chief-of-staff in 1938. He became the US Army's chief-of-staff shortly before the outbreak of World War II in Europe and immediately set about the daunting task of vastly expanding the 200,000-strong army, which eventually totaled some eight million men.

He also undertook a major root-and-branch reform of its organization by creating three separate commands—Army Ground Forces, Army Service Forces, and Army Air Forces from 1942—to improve efficiency. Marshall was also a member of the Joint Chiefs-of-Staff and, as Roosevelt's main military adviser, attended many major Allied planning conferences. He had many outstanding qualities, not least his organizational skills and, although he didn't become as well known as more flamboyant figures, there is no doubt that Marshall was one of the main architects of the final Allied victory, not least for turning the US Army into a war-fighting machine.

Left: Marshall was Roosevelt's chief adviser on matters pertaining to the military.

Mitscher, Marc

(1887–1947) Nationality: American.
Senior position: Deputy Chief of Naval Operations (Air).
Final rank: Vice-Admiral.

Mitscher, who graduated from the Naval Academy in 1910, was an early pioneer of naval aviation. He served in several increasingly senior positions during the interwar years, becoming assistant chief to the Bureau of Aeronautics in

Below: Mitscher (center right) poses with Doolittle and other volunteers shortly before the long-range bombing raid on the Japanese mainland, April 1942.

Mikawa, Guinichi

(1888–1981) Nationality: Japanese.
Senior position: Commander Eighth Fleet.
Final rank: Vice-Admiral.

Mikawa took part in the attack on Pearl Harbor in December 1941, an operation in which he led the Support Force. He then took charge of a fleet based at Rabaul in the Southwest Pacific and became embroiled in a number of naval battles off Guadalcanal during 1942. He was later based in the Philippines in command of both air and naval forces.

Above: Mikawa sank four US cruisers at the Battle of Savo Island.

1939. Two years later he was posted to the new carrier *Hornet* and brought it into commission during October. He commanded the carrier when it undertook the Doolittle Raid on mainland Japan in April 1942 and captained the same warship during the Battle of Midway in June.

After a spell on land directing operations on Guadalcanal, he returned to sea in command of a task force, and took part in operations against the Marshalls, Truk, and New Guinea during the first half of 1944. He directed carrier operations during the decisive Battle of the Philippine Sea in June and then supported landings on the Bonins, Palau, and Leyte. In the latter case he scored a notable victory during the Battle of Leyte Gulf. In the final year of the war he served at Iwo Jima and Okinawa before returning home to a senior staff command in July.

Model, Walther

(1891–1945) Nationality: German:'
Senior position: Commander-in-Chief West.
Final rank: Field Marshal.

Model, who was a member of the Nazi Party, first gained a reputation for competence in the early campaigns of World War II. He led the Sixteenth Army during the invasion of France and the Low Countries and then led the 3rd Panzer

Above: Model was nicknamed the "Fuehrer's Fireman" because of his ability to resolve seemingly impossible military problems.

Division during the 1941 invasion of the Soviet Union. He served on the Eastern Front until late summer 1944 and during that time he gained more and more senior commands. He led the northern pincer of the unsuccessful German offensive against the Kursk salient in July 1943, and then commanded Army Group North in the first three months of 1944.

In late June he was given charge of what was left of Army Group Center, which had recently been largely shattered by a Soviet offensive, and then had to deal with the fall-out from the July Bomb Plot that had come close to killing Hitler. Model immediately professed his loyalty and was given charge of Army Group B. More promotions followed and he was made commander of all the German forces in Western Europe on 17 August. He skillfully dealt with the Allied airborne assault on Arnhem in September and led the ultimately unsuccessful Ardennes offensive. His luck was, however, running out and he and some 300,000 German troops were surrounded in the Ruhr Pocket in April 1945. Rather than surrender personally, he committed suicide.

Below: Model (right) holds discussions with a fellow officer during a lull in the fighting on the Eastern Front.

Montgomery, Bernard
(1887–1976) Nationality: British.
Senior position: Commander 21st Army Group.
Final rank: Field Marshal.

Montgomery graduated from Sandhurst military academy in 1908 and then served as a junior officer in an infantry regiment. During World War I he fought on the Western Front, being badly wounded in late 1914, and also served as

Above: Montgomery poses for a photograph during the fighting in the Western Desert.

a staff officer with various large formations after his recovery. During the interwar years he attended staff college and, after a spell on routine duties in Britain, returned there as an instructor in early 1926. Much of the 1930s were spent overseas in Egypt, India, and Palestine. He returned home in late 1939 and, when war broke out, he sailed to France as a divisional commander with the British Expeditionary Force.

Montgomery came to wider notice thanks to the way he handled the rear guard during the generally chaotic retreat to the Dunkirk perimeter in May-June 1940. He escaped back to Britain and was given command of V Corps, stationed in southern England, the following month and was then posted to take charge of another corps in April 1941. The following November he was promoted to command the whole Southeastern Army and, while in this position, he was involved in planning the unsuccessful Dieppe Raid. The assault on the French resort actually took place in August 1942 but by this stage Montgomery was preparing to take charge of the First Army for the forthcoming Allied landings in French North Africa, code-named Operation Torch.

He was, however, fated to take charge of the Eighth Army in Egypt after its commander had died in August. Italian and German forces were at the gates of Egypt and close to reaching the strategically vital Suez Canal, but Montgomery was narrowly able to halt their advance at the Battle of Alam Halfa in the first week of September. He then steadily built up his own forces, received fresh equipment and, perhaps most importantly of all, set about rebuilding his troops' morale and self-belief. The fruits of all of this work plus detailed planning came with victory at the Second Battle of El Alamein, which began on 23 October. It was not, in World War II terms, a large battle, and it was won only after some hard fighting, but it was decisive. Montgomery's opponents were in retreat, even though he was criticized by some for not pressing them hard enough after the battle was declared over on 4 November.

Montgomery now pressed westwards towards Tunisia as mainly US forces pushed eastwards from their Torch landing beaches. He repulsed a German attack at Medenine in March 1943 but was in turn given a bloody nose at Mareth in March. But he was eventually able to outflank the enemy position by early April. The Tunisian campaign ended in May and Montgomery next led the Eighth Army during the Sicily campaign, which reached a success-

Above: A battlefield conference between Montgomery (center, pointing) and several of his corps and divisional commanders during the Second Battle of El Alamein in late 1942.
Right: A rare moment of calm between Montgomery and Patton—in reality, they loathed each other.

ful conclusion by August. Patton was also on the island and the two, who were both willful and somewhat egocentric, further developed their dislike for each other. It was an animosity that would continue for the remainder of the war.

Montgomery led the Eighth Army during the early

stages of the campaign on the Italian mainland but left his old command to return to Britain to lead the 21st Army Group during the invasion of Western Europe. He was also made commander-in-chief ground forces and thus oversaw most of the bitter and unproductive fighting in Normandy during July and early August 1944. He kept the latter post until the arrival of Eisenhower on 1 September and thereafter concentrated on the army group until the war's end. Montgomery was usually a cautious commander but he next planned at short notice Operation Market Garden, a bold plan to grab bridges over various rivers in Holland during September, as a prelude to a swift push into Germany's industrial heartland.

Below: Montgomery celebrated the completion of the 1,000th pre-fabricated Bailey Bridge built by the British since the D-Day landings.

The airborne raid was a costly fiasco and Eisenhower decided to continue his previous broad-front strategy until Germany had been defeated, but Montgomery's army group on the northern shoulder of the advance began to play a subsidiary role in operations. He did participate in the defeat of the German Ardennes offensive at the end of the year but somewhat overstated his role in it at various media conferences, much to the chagrin of senior US commanders. Montgomery did well during the crossing of the River Rhine in March and then pushed into northern Germany, where he accepted the surrender of German forces in Holland and northwest Germany on 4 May. He then commanded the British occupation forces until 1946.

Below: Montgomery discusses matters with two of his officers— Horrocks (center), a corps commander, and Thomas, who had charge of a division—"somewhere in Northwest Europe."

Morshead, Leslie

(1889–1959) Nationality: Australian.
Senior position: Commander Second Army.
Final rank: Lieutenant-General.

Morshead commanded the Australian 9th Division during the North Africa campaign, in which it successfully defended Tobruk in 1941 and fought at the Second Battle of El Alamein, and then in Papua New Guinea. He was made commander of the New Guinea force in 1944 and led an army before ending the war in Borneo.

Above: Morshead was a tough, hard-driving commander, who was nicknamed by his own troops "Ming the Merciless."

Mountbatten, Louis

(1900–1979) Nationality: British.
Senior position: Commander-in-chief Southeast Asia
  Area.
Final rank: Vice-Admiral.

Mountbatten commanded the 5th Destroyer Flotilla in 1939 and fought in Norway and the Mediterranean, losing his own warship in May 1941 off Crete. He then worked in Combined Operations and in 1943 was given charge of a Far Eastern command. He accepted the Japanese surrender in Singapore in September 1945.

Above: Known as a problem-solver, Mountbatten also believed in the use of cutting-edge science and technology in warfare.

Mussolini, Benito

(1883–1945) Nationality: Italian.
Senior position: Italian Dictator.

Born in northern Italy, Mussolini briefly studied for life as a schoolteacher in his early adulthood, but then fled to Switzerland in 1902 to avoid compulsory military service. He had a change of heart while in exile and returned to his homeland and entered the military two years later. He next worked as unskilled labor and became active in the socialist movement, becoming editor of *Avanti*, the official organ of the Italian Socialist Party, in 1912. He left the movement

Above: Mussolini with his German rescuers, September 1943, after the Italian dictator had been overthrown.

in 1915 as his former colleagues wished to keep Italy out of World War I, a position he strongly disagreed with. He fought in the conflict as a corporal, was invalided out after being wounded, and began editing a

Below: Hitler was an admirer of Mussolini but the latter increasingly became the junior partner in their alliance once the war had begun.

populist rightwing newspaper, *Il Popolo di Italia.*

Mussolini now created the Fascist Party out of various like-minded groups and it did well in early postwar elections, so much so that by 1922 his demands for a fascist government were agreed. Amidst a background of much social unrest, Mussolini became prime minister and conducted the much-mythologized

"March on Rome" to take power— most of the journey from Milan was actually undertaken by train and the march was little more than a pre-planned celebratory parade not a bold seizure of power. He now attempted to remold Italy to recreate a facsimile of its ancient imperial past, with emphasis on national pride, military might, and absolute obedience to the new leader—Il Duce.

Above: Hitler and Mussolini attend military maneuvers in 1937, during the Italian leader's state visit to Nazi Germany.

Italy was thus transformed into a one-party state as socialists and other opponents were dealt with ruthlessly. Power was exercised through the Fascist Grand Council but it did little more than rubber stamp Mussolini's own policies. Although much exaggerated by fascist propaganda, these policies did help many ordinary Italians and inspired other rightwing leaders, not least Hitler. The two dictators moved closer together during the 1930s, although Mussolini rather distrusted the German dictator in their early meetings. Nevertheless, signs of cooperation between the two emerged with the signing of the Axis alliance in late 1936, although Hitler increasingly became the dominant partner.

Italy annexed Albania in 1939 and the same year Mussolini and Hitler signed a defensive military alliance known as the Pact of Steel. Mussolini rapidly grew to envy Hitler's conquests in the early stages of World War II and in June 1940 he declared war against the Allies, even though Italy was in no way prepared to conduct large-scale military operations or support them economically. What followed was a series of disastrous military campaigns in Egypt, East Africa, and Greece, as well as at sea in the Mediterranean, that shattered Mussolini's imperial ambitions. From 1941 he and Italy itself were overwhelmingly reliant on the German military machine and its own economy was floundering.

Despite these harsh realities, Mussolini continued to act as Hitler's equal—he made an enemy out of the Soviet Union by sending troops to the Eastern Front, and declared war on the United States in late 1941. Not until late 1942, when Axis fortunes in North Africa deteriorated significantly, did the dictator begin to appreciate the severity of the situation, nor did he appreciate his own perilous situation. The war had never been especially popular among the wider Italian population and even the king and other senior statesmen were looking at ways to remove Mussolini from power.

Mussolini's downfall began shortly after he met with Hitler in northern Italy during July 1943. When he returned to Rome, he found the king, the Fascist Grand Council, and leading figures in the military demanding that he resign. He had little option but to agree and was placed under house arrest in a remote mountaintop hotel. Salvation seemingly came in September when he was rescued by a small force of German troops led by Otto Skorzeny (whom Churchill had dubbed the "most dangerous man in Europe") and flown to Germany. Hitler allowed him to set up the Salo Republic in German-controlled northern Italy, but such a puppet mini-state was no more than a salve to Mussolini's pride. He did have his revenge, though, when five of those involved in his downfall faced a show trial and were unsurprisingly shot.

The end came for Mussolini in April 1945 as Allied troops advanced through northern Italy. He attempted to flee to Switzerland with his mistress, Clara Petacci, but they were intercepted by Italian partisans near Lake Como on the 27 April. They were executed the following day and put on public display in Milan. Mussolini was in many ways vulgar and brash and not averse to using violence to achieve his political goals, but he was not born out of the same mould as Hitler. He was delusional in many of the same ways as his Nazi counterpart, but not genocidal.

Nagumo, Chuichi
(1887–1944) Nationality: Japanese.
Senior Position: Commander First Carrier Strike Force.
Final rank: Vice-Admiral.

Nagumo led Japan's main carrier fleet in offensives across the Pacific between December 1941 and June1942, but Midway showed that he was not suited to their operations. After further failures off Guadalcanal, he was moved sideways before taking over the garrison on Saipan. He committed suicide when the island was overrun in 1944.

Above: Nagumo's greatest mistake was to call off a third strike by his carriers during the attack on Pearl Harbor, 7 December 1941.

Nimitz, Chester

(1885–1966) Nationality: American.
Senior position: Commander Pacific Ocean Area.
Final rank: Fleet Admiral.

Nimitz attended the US Navy's college at Annapolis between 1901 and 1905 and then served on submarines, becoming the chief-of-staff to the commander of the Atlantic Fleet submarine force during 1917-1919. During the interwar period he held a number of staff posts, undertook further training, chiefly at the Naval War College (1922-1923) and, as the war clouds gathered in the late 1930s, commanded first a cruiser and then a battleship division with the rank of rear-admiral.

By June 1939 Nimitz was head of the Bureau of Navigation, a body tasked with recruiting and training both officers and enlisted men for the rapidly expanding navy. The Japanese attack on Pearl Harbor on 7 December 1941 led to the relief of the then-commander-in-chief of the Pacific Fleet some ten days later, and Nimitz became his successor on the last day of the year. His immediate work was devoted to protecting the highly vulnerable Hawaiian Islands but in March 1942 he was also given greater responsibility when he was named commander of all the armed forces—land, sea, and air—in the so-called Pacific Ocean Area.

Nimitz's immediate aim was to defend what remained of the US positions in the Pacific and maintain communications with the continental United States, Australia, and India. The Battle of the Coral Sea in May effectively stopped Japan's long series of offensives that had been initiated by the attack on Pearl Harbor. The Battle of Midway in June then ensured that the US forces held the initiative in the Pacific after severe losses were inflicted on Japan's elite carrier force and its highly trained pilots. Henceforth, Nimitz would go over to the offensive, while the Japanese largely remained on the defensive. To aid the forthcoming campaign, he wholly reorganized the Allied forces stationed in the vast theater of operations, which stretched from the borders of Burma and India to the Aleutians, into a number of separate commands. Although

Neurath, Konstantin von

(1873–1956) Nationality: German.
Senior position: Reich Protector of Bohemia-Moravia.

Neurath, a conservative rather than a Nazi by conviction, was Hitler's foreign minister from 1932 to 1938. Between 1939 and 1941 he ruled over Bohemia-Moravia, a puppet regime established in part of Czechoslovakia, but was replaced when he failed to implement Nazi policies. He was sentenced to 15 years' imprisonment at Nuremberg.

Above: Neurath served as Germany's foreign minister for much of the 1930s, but was largely used to hide their radical policies.

Left: Nimitz (center) pays a visit to one of the Pacific islands his amphibious task forces have just wrestled from the Japanese.
Above: Nimitz (right) poses with Roosevelt and MacArthur. The two military men frequently argued about the allocation of resources but Nimitz was usually given priority.

all of these would see fighting to a lesser or greater extent, those zones designated the Central Pacific and Southwest Pacific Areas would be critical to the defeat of Japan.

His subsequent strategy was based on a two-pronged converging drive directed toward the Japanese home islands by these two forces. Aircraft carriers and Marine-

dominated amphibious expeditionary forces island-hopped their way through the Central Pacific, while land-based aircraft and shorter-range amphibious assaults by mostly army units carved a path northward through the Southwest Pacific. The eventual aim was to link up in the Philippines before tackling Japan itself. Although there was friction

between the two commands over the allocation of resources, the strategy was fundamentally sound.

MacArthur, who commanded in the southwest and began offensive operations with landings on Guadalcanal in early August 1942, made steady progress through the rest of the Solomons, while the forces of the Central Pacific Area leapfrogged between islands groups. Nimitz, who had to assemble the vast naval resources to conduct such complex, long-range invasions almost from scratch, began somewhat later by tackling the Gilberts in November1943, then the Marshalls in spring 1944, and next the Marianas and Palaus during the following summer-fall. Nimitz held operational command in each of these amphibious operations but allowed a number of "fighting" admirals of mostly sound judgment to have tactical control over the actual combat. Many painful, costly lessons were learned, especially on Tarawa in the Gilberts, but the problems relating to tactics and appropriate equipment were soon ironed out. Critically, the huge amphibious task forces were split into various sub-divisions— such as carrier strike forces, bombardment groups, amphibious assault units, and supply flotillas—that had clearly defined but inter-related missions. Carrier strike forces, for example, were often sent ahead to soften up a target, while the bombardment groups operated a little before and during the actual landings proper.

The Central and Southwest Pacific Area forces linked up in October 1944 to invade the Philippines but Nimitz next used Central Pacific Area forces to attack Iwo Jima and then Okinawa in the first half of 1945. These were two of the toughest landings of the entire campaign, but he prevailed and was left standing within striking distance of the Japanese home islands. As the war entered its final phases, he directed operations against Japan itself but the need to invade evaporated after atomic bombs were dropped on Hiroshima and Nagasaki in August. Nimitz's final act of the war was to witness the signing of the official surrender documents on USS *Missouri*, in Tokyo Bay on 2 September.

Nomura, Kichisaburo

(1877–1964) Nationality: Japanese.
Senior position: Ambassador to the United States.
Final rank: Admiral.

Nomura was made his country's foreign minister in 1939 but then accepted the post of ambassador to the United States. He held various fruitless discussions with the US secretary of state right up to the eve of war but was repatriated after Pearl Harbor on 7 December 1941 (whether he was aware of it is a moot point) and tended his resignation.

Left: US Marines unload supplies directly onto the beach of Iwo Jima during one of the bitterest battles of the entire Pacific campaign.

Above: Nomura served with the Imperial Japanese Navy before embarking on a career as a diplomat.

O'Connor, Richard

(1889–1981) Nationality: British.
Senior position: General Officer Commanding British
   Forces Egypt.
Final rank: General.

Oldendorf, Jesse

(1887–1974) Nationality: American.
Senior position: Commander Combat Formations
   Seventh Fleet.
Final rank: Rear Admiral.

O'Connor became head of the Western Desert Force that attacked the Italians in late 1940 and by early 1941 had decisively defeated them. He was made commander of British forces in Egypt but was captured in March. Incarcerated in Italy until December 1943, he returned to service to lead a corps during the liberation of Western Europe in 1944–1945.

Oldendorf served in the Caribbean and Atlantic between January 1942 and December 1943 and then operated in the Pacific as a US task group commander in operations against the Marshalls, Marianas, and Leyte Gulf in 1944. During the latter action he scored a key victory at night in the Surigao Strait, and also fought at Okinawa in 1945.

Above: O'Connor (left) discusses military matters with his superior, Wavell, commander-in-chief of the Middle East and North Africa.

Above: Oldendorf's command bore the brunt of Japanese *kamikaze* attacks during the fighting off Luzon in January 1945.

Onishi, Takijiro

(1891–1945) Nationality: Japanese.
Senior position: Commander Special Attack Group.
Final rank: Admiral.

Onishi was the chief-of-staff of Japan's Eleventh Air Fleet in 1941 and, with fellow officers, carried out a feasibility study for the attack on Pearl Harbor. By 1944 he was commanding a mere 100 aircraft on Luzon and established the first *kamikaze* unit. Unable to deal with defeat, he committed suicide in August 1945.

Above: Onishi was a fanatical nationalist and was held in high regard by the staff that surrounded him.

Oppenheimer, Robert

(1904–1967) Nationality: American.
Final position: Head of Research Los Alamos.

Although he ultimately had doubts about the morality of using atomic weapons, Oppenheimer was the key scientist in the Manhattan Project. A professor of atomic physics at the University of California, he was made director of the Los Alamos laboratory and head of the group building the first such bomb in 1942.

Above: Oppenheimer was a brilliant scientist but was ambivalent about the atomic bomb project.

Ozawa, Jisaburo

(1896–1966) Nationality: Japanese.
Senior position: Vice-Chief Naval General Staff.
Final rank: Vice-Admiral.

Ozawa commanded the Mobile Fleet from 1942 until 1945 but did not take charge of the fast-dwindling carrier force until March 1944. He saw the loss of three carriers and virtually all of their aircraft at the Battle of the Philippine Sea the following June and saw the destruction of what remained at the Battle of Cape Engano on 25 October.

Left: A Japanese aircraft dives to destruction, narrowly missing a US aircraft carrier.

Park, Keith

(1892–1975) Nationality: New Zealander.
Senior position: Air Commander-in-Chief Southeast Asia Command.
Final rank: Air Chief Marshal.

Park led a fighter group during the Battle of Britain and between 1941 and 1943 was the senior air officer in Egypt and Malta. He organized support for the North Africa landings as well as those on Sicily and the Italian mainland. In early 1944 he became supreme air commander in the Middle East and was based in the Far East from February 1945.

Above: Keith Park played a key role in the Battle of Britain, commanding the fighter force in the vulnerable southeast of England.

Above: Park (left, with Dowding) played a key role in covering the mass evacuation from Dunkirk in 1940.

Patch, Alexander, Jr.

(1889–1945) Nationality: American.
Senior position: Commander Seventh Army.
Final rank: Lieutenant-General.

Patch was commander of the Infantry Replacement Center in 1941 but then led a division during the latter stage of the battle for Guadalcanal in late 1942 to early 1943. Thereafter he fought in Europe at the head of the Seventh Army, which landed in southern France in August 1944 and then fought its way northwards and eastwards into Germany.

Above: Patch (second from left) poses for a photograph with other senior figures, including Secretary of the Navy Forrestal (second from right), shortly before the invasion of southern France, 1944.

Patton, George

(1885–1945) Nationality: American.
Senior position: Commander Third Army.
Final rank: Major-General.

Patton was born into an old military family and studied at both the Virginia Military Institute and West Point. He saw service in the expedition into Mexico in pursuit of Pancho Villa in 1916–1917 and then went to France, where he set up the US tank training school. He saw action with an armored brigade in the final offensives on the Western Front and then returned home. During the 1920s he held a variety of posts in the much-reduced army, both as a commanding officer of cavalry units and on the staff.

In July 1941, after a stint commanding the 3rd Cavalry, Patton was placed in charge of the 2nd Armored Brigade,

Left: Patton, seen here during prewar maneuvers, became a master of armored warfare and honed his skills when acting and actual commander of the US 2nd Armored Division during 1940–1941.

Above: Patton receives a ticker-tape welcome as he parades through the streets of New York at the end of the war.

which was redesignated a division the following November. He and his unit performed well during maneuvers that summer and fall, and he was made commander of I Armored Corps in January 1942. He next spent a period as head of the Desert Training Center and then took part in the planning for Operation Torch, the Allied landings at various points in French-controlled North Africa.

Patton successfully led the Western Task Force ashore at several points on the Moroccan coast on 8 November and in March 1943 was given command of the US II Corps after both it units and its commanding officer had performed badly at the Battle of Kasserine Pass in Tunisia. The general was briefly relieved of command after a squabble with the British but was reinstated to take charge of I Armored Corps, which was expanded and renamed the US

Seventh Army in July.

Patton led the Seventh Army with considerable spirit and drive during the Sicilian campaign in July and August but on 16 August he became embroiled in a damaging incident when he slapped and threatened to shoot a shell-shocked soldier in a field hospital after accusing him of rank cowardice. This became public knowledge and he was ordered by Eisenhower to make a public apology to each and every unit under his

Left: Patton confers with Mountbatten in England during August 1943, shortly before taking part in Operation Torch.

Above: The general presents an award to a chaplain from a unit serving with his US Third Army in Northwest Europe, 1944–1945.

command. Patton's career was blighted and for the next several months he had little to do but bide his time and await reassignment.

Salvation came in January 1944 when he went to England and was given command of the newly arrived US Third Army. Patton reached France a month or so after the D-Day landings of 6 June, a time when the Allies were mostly bogged down and making virtually no progress. When the breakout came, it was spearheaded by the Third Army, which first pushed into Brittany and then turned east for a lightning dash across France that was eventually marred by supply problems. Patton was close to the German border by the end of the year but then came the Ardennes Offensive to his north on 16 December. He immediately swung his army through ninety degrees and threw it into the battle, relieving the vital town of Bastogne on the 26th.

Patton's forces slogged their way to the River Rhine in the first three months of 1945 but he then threw some units across the barrier at Oppenheim on 2 March, although ordered not to do so, and this opened the way into the heartland of Nazi Germany. German resistance was by now crumbling and Patton's armored columns were soon rushing at will through the southern part of the country. They then pushed into northern Bavaria and by the end of the war were in parts of Czechoslovakia. Patton was subsequently removed from his governorship of Bavaria and command of the Third Army for his outspokenness regarding the Allied de-Nazification program. He died after complications set in after a car accident on 9 December.

Patton was without doubt the finest offensive-minded general that the western Allies could field. He was a master of fast-moving armored warfare in the mold of Rommel and was one of the few Allied generals that the Germans truly feared. He was at heart a traditionalist whose bluntness could shock those who did not know him well. He also a great self-publicist—he liked to be seen wearing a pair of pearl-handled revolvers and had an eye for a favorable photo-opportunity—who had the unfortunate habit of getting himself into trouble on several occasions. Equally, the mutual loathing between Patton and Montgomery was a not very well kept secret. Yet for all his faults, Patton was the western Allies' best army commander of the war.

Paulus, Friedrich

(1890–1957) Nationality: German.
Senior position: Commander Sixth Army.
Final rank: Field Marshal.

Paulus, who had served as a junior officer in World War I, first made his mark as a staff officer with the Tenth (later Sixth) Army during its successful campaigns in Poland, Belgium, and France during 1939 and 1940. He was then promoted to become deputy chief-of-staff, operation section, of the high command and was set to work to study

Above: Paulus was the only German field marshal ever to have surrendered to the enemy.

the feasibility of invading the Soviet Union. Operation Barbarossa went ahead in June 1941 and in January of the following year Paulus returned to his old army but as its commander. He was ordered to drive towards the River Volga and take Stalingrad.

Paulus did reach Stalingrad but soon became embroiled in bitter street-fighting. Much of the city was captured but its garrison held out until a Red Army counterattack in November surrounded the Sixth Army in turn. Paulus was ordered to stand fast but all efforts at relief failed and he surrendered along with some 90,000 troops on 2 February 1943, a day after he had been promoted to field marshal by Hitler. He was imprisoned in Moscow but began broadcasting anti-Nazi radio messages from mid-1944.

Pétain, Henri

(1856–1951) Nationality: French.
Senior position: President of Vichy France.
Final rank: Marshal.

World War I hero Pétain became French president in June 1940 and was then head of the collaborationist Vichy French government. His powers declined as the war progressed, especially after the Vichy-controlled part of France was occupied by the Germans in late 1942. Tried for treason, his death sentence was commuted to life imprisonment.

Above: Pétain was a World War I hero, but his actions during World War II led to him being viewed as a traitor.

Portal, Charles

(1893–1971) Nationality: British.
Senior position: Chief of Air Staff.
Final rank: Air Chief Marshal.

Pound, Dudley

(1877–1943) Nationality: British.
Senior position: First Sea Lord.
Final rank: Admiral.

Portal was head of RAF Bomber Command until 1940, when he became chief of the Air Staff. He was an advocate of strategic bombing but believed that area rather than precision bombing was the only way to prosecute the campaign. As the war progressed he argued, with slight success, that bombers should mainly support ground operations.

Above: Portal directed a sizeable part of Bomber Command's strength to attack German communications centers in the run-up to D-Day.

Pound was made first sea lord and promoted admiral in 1939, and he also chaired the British Chiefs-of-Staff Committee. His was very much a hands-on approach and his judgment was usually sound, although his decision to allow a convoy to Russia to scatter in July 1942 was much criticized. Pound resigned his post through illness.

Above: Pound was a hands-on first sea lord and his unjustifiable interventions on operational matters drew considerable criticism.

Quezon, Manuel
(1878–1944) Nationality: Filipino.
Senior position: President of the Philippines.

Quisling, Vidkun
(1887–1945) Nationality: Norwegian.
Senior position: Minister President.

Quezon served as president from 1933, and was a staunch supporter of his country's close ties with the United States. He remained in his country when the Japanese invaded in 1941 but was eventually evacuated to Australia in 1942, and from there traveled to the United States. He never lived to see his homeland's liberation.

Above: Quezon died from tuberculosis a mere three months before his homeland was liberated.

Quisling was an ex-officer in the Norwegian Army and had served as a government minister before forming the *Nasjonal Samling*, a right-wing political party with strong Nazi sympathies. He became head of a puppet regime after the Germans invaded. He was arrested on 9 May 1945, tried for treason, and hanged.

Above: Quisling's name became synonymous with treachery after he formed a pro-Nazi Finnish government.

Raeder, Erich

**(1876–1960) Nationality: German.
Senior position: Commander-in-
Chief Kriegsmarine.
Final rank: Grand Admiral.**

Raeder joined the Imperial German
Navy in 1894 and saw service during
World War I in staff posts and during
offensive operations at sea, most
notably taking part in hit-and-run
raids on the coast of England. He
stayed in the much-reduced navy
during the interwar years during
which he wrote a volume on cruiser
warfare. Raeder was successively
promoted to vice-admiral in 1925 and
to admiral in 1928, when he was also
made chief of the Naval Command. It
was during this period that he set
about modernizing and expanding the
navy in direct contravention of the
Treaty of Versailles.

He stayed in the service when the
Nazis assumed power in 1933 and he
was made its commander-in-chief in
1935. He then embarked on Plan Z, an
ultimately uncompleted secret plan
that had been devised to make
Germany a naval superpower by 1944
or 1945. However, when war broke
out in 1939 it was effectively
cancelled with much of the construction work either uncompleted or still
on the drawing board. Raeder eventually gave his support to all-out subma-

Right: Raeder wanted to build a major
battle fleet but he actually oversaw the
development of one more appropriate to
commerce-raiding duties.

rine warfare but also firmly believed that the navy still needed a sizeable surface fleet. This position led to arguments with his peers, many of whom felt that such costly warships were an unnecessary luxury.

As the war progressed the navy's larger surface warships did not perform particularly well and several of them, like *Graf Spee* in 1939 and *Bismarck* in 1941, were lost. Hitler increasingly put his faith in the more successful U-boats, turning his back on the surface fleet and Raeder. These events plus other disagreements on maritime strategy ultimately led to Raeder's dismissal in January 1943. Captured at the war's end, he was sentenced to life imprisonment at Nuremberg but released after nine years.

Left: Raeder, who welcomed Hitler's rise to power, is seen here in discussion with a pair of senior army officers during a rally at Nuremberg.

Below: By the outbreak of the war, Germany's navy had grown from a small coastal defense force into a powerful, modern fleet, although its major warships, including *Graf Spee*, shown here) did not perform well.

Ramsey, Bertram

**(1883–1945) Nationality: British.
Senior position: Naval Commander-
in-Chief D-Day.
Final rank: Admiral.**

Ramsey served with the Grand Fleet during World War I but retired from the service in 1938, only to be recalled in August the following year. As the flag officer at Dover, he master-minded the Anglo-French evacuation from Dunkirk in 1940, and this face-saving success led to him being appointed as naval force commander in 1942 for the eventual invasion of occupied Europe. However, D-Day lay some time in the future; he also played a major role in the Allied landings in Algeria in 1942, where he was deputy commander of the Eastern Task Force, and the Sicily invasion of July 1943.

Ramsey returned to England the following November and was promoted to naval commander-in-chief for the D-Day landings. Ramsey, who was widely respected by his peers, once again showed his caliber: the complex amphibious landings during Operation Neptune on 6 June were an organizational triumph. Thereafter he planned the naval assault on the island of Walcheren, but Ramsey did not see the final defeat of Nazi Germany as he was killed in an air crash on 2 January 1945 while traveling to Brussels for a meeting with Montgomery.

Above: Ramsey (left) watches the Allied armada leave England to begin the liberation of Western Europe, June 1944.

Ribbentrop, Joachim von

(1893–1946) Nationality: German.
Senior position: Foreign Minister.

Ridgway, Matthew

(1895–1993) Nationality: American.
Senior position: Commander XVIII Airborne Corps.
Final rank: Lieutenant-General.

Ribbentrop was a vain man ("von" was an undeserved aristocratic affectation) with few social graces or diplomatic skills. Hitler made him his foreign minister in 1938. He signed the German-Soviet Non-Aggression Pact in 1939, but he was increasingly sidelined by Hitler. Captured by the Allies in 1945, he was tried at Nuremburg and hanged.

Above: Although ostensibly Nazi Germany's foreign minister, Ribbentrop did not initiate the diplomacy with which he was involved.

Ridgway, an exponent of airborne warfare, commanded the US 82nd Airborne Division for the invasion of Sicily in 1943. After a spell fighting on the Italian mainland, his command took part in the Normandy landings. He then took over an airborne corps for operations in Holland and also fought in the Ardennes as well as at the Rhine and Elbe crossings.

Above: Ridgway, seen here meeting Montgomery, was the most senior US airborne commander of the war.

Ritchie, Neil

(1897–1983) Nationality: British.
Senior position: Commander Eighth Army.
Final rank: General.

After spells as a staff officer in Europe and the Middle East, Ritchie took command of the British forces in Egypt in November 1941, but the bad situation there was made worse in January 1942 when Rommel launched a successful counterattack that saw the fall of Tobruk. Ritchie was sacked in June but ably commanded a corps in Europe after D-Day.

Above: Ritchie fell out of favor following defeat at the Battle of Gazala and the fall of Tobruk in June 1942.

Rokossovsky, Konstantin

(1896–1968) Nationality: Russian.
Senior position: Commander Stalingrad Front.
Final rank: Marshal.

Rokossovsky was an outstanding army group commander who distinguished himself in the Ukraine and outside Moscow in 1941, at Stalingrad in 1942, and at Kursk in 1943. He subsequently led the drive towards and eventual capture of Warsaw in1944, and then swept north to trap the German garrison of East Prussia by early 1945.

Above: Controversially, Rokossovsky halted his forces for several months outside Warsaw in 1944.

penned *Infanterie Greift An* (*Infantry Attacks*) in 1937. He commanded Hitler's personal bodyguard from 1938 and was personally responsible for the *Fuehrer*'s security during the invasion of Poland in 1939. He was next given command of the 7th Panzer Division for the invasion of

Rommel, Erwin

(1891–1944) Nationality: German.
Senior position: Commander Army Group B.
Final rank: Field Marshal.

Rommel was a much-decorated veteran of World War I who remained in the much-reduced army during the inter-war years. He was also something of a military theorist and

Above: Rommel strikes a suitably martial pose before attending a conference.
Right: Rommel, the "Desert Fox," discusses matters with Kesselring (left), the *Luftwaffe*'s commander in southern Europe.

France and the Low Countries in May 1940 and performed with undoubted skill. His drive to the Channel won Hitler's favor and in early 1941 he was given command of what would become the *Deutsches Afrika Korps* and sent to North Africa to aid the collapsing Italians.

He quickly transformed the situation and over the next several months

Above: Various officers attend a planning meeting authorized by Rommel (second from right) in the Western Desert.

engaged in a series of see-saw campaigns across the Western Desert that greatly if somewhat excessively further enhanced his reputation. There were several notable victories, not least the capture of Tobruk in June 1942. However, he was

Right: Rommel, seen here during the invasion of France in 1940, shot to fame as the commander of the 7th Panzer Division.
Below: Despite the inherent dangers, Rommel was a commander who liked to lead from the front.

decisively beaten at the Second Battle of Alamein, which began the following October, and thereafter fought a largely defensive campaign along the borders of Tunisia until ordered home in March 1943 just a few months before the North African campaign ended in defeat for the Axis powers.

After a spell in northern Italy, Rommel was put in charge of the German forces garrisoning the Low Countries and northern France in January 1944. Despite Rommel's efforts to strengthen the Atlantic Wall, it was still incomplete by the time of the Allied Normandy landings in June and his army group failed to throw the Allies back into the sea. Rommel himself was badly wounded on 17 July when his staff car was strafed by a fighter, and he did not serve at the front again. Implicated in the anti-

Above: A scene from the North African campaign—Rommel instructs one of his commanders.

Hitler Bomb Plot—although the extent of his involvement is a matter of conjecture—he chose suicide the following October rather than see his family sent to a concentration camp. Hitler granted the fallen field marshal a state funeral.

Roosevelt, Franklin

(1882–1945) Nationality: American. Senior position: President of the United States.

Roosevelt was a Democrat politician with a distinguished political lineage who overcame physical disability brought about by a severe attack of polio in 1921 to achieve his nation's highest office. The attack was so debilitating that he did not return to action until 1928 yet he was still elected president in 1933, the year the Nazis came to power. Roosevelt spent most of the years before the outbreak of World War II in 1939 dragging the United States out of the Great Depression thanks to the various economic and financial programs collectively known as the "New Deal." When war broke out in Europe that September he faced a delicate balancing act. He was acutely aware that few of his fellow countrymen and women felt that the United States should become embroiled in a seemingly distant conflict, yet he also believed that Nazi Germany, a tyranny of the sort he deplored, could not be allowed to defeat Britain and its Allies. Roosevelt therefore began to move his country slowly but surely ever closer to Britain.

He also set about preparing his homeland for war and embarked on an unprecedented expansion of the country's comparatively small armed forces. Indeed, he was persuasive enough to get Congress to agree the first peacetime conscription bill, the Selective Service Act, in the country's history during September 1940, but still stated publicly that he would not lead the United States into war. Roosevelt also aided the Allies, especially Britain, which by this stage of the war was effectively on its own. One scheme was the destroyers-for-bases deal agreed in the same month in which the Royal Navy received fifty much-needed if outdated destroyers in return for giving the United States ninety-nine-year leases on certain bases in the Caribbean. Further, the Lend-Lease Act of March 1941 insured that Britain would receive vital war supplies.

Left: Roosevelt photographed in 1930 when he was governor of New York; he won his first presidential race in 1932.

Right: Architects of the "special relationship," Roosevelt and Churchill, along with their military staffs, attended the Casablanca Conference in January 1943.

Roosevelt also struck up a close relationship with Churchill, with whom he agreed a common set of war aims, known as the Atlantic Charter, at a meeting in Placentia Bay, Newfoundland, the following August. The turning point came on 7 December when the Japanese surprise attack on Pearl Harbor decisively silenced the country's anti-war isolationists. It was followed by German and Italian declarations of

figure at home, winning a fourth landslide victory in 1944, and mostly avoided any damaging rifts between Democrats and Republicans. He also showed a deft hand on the international stage, attending numerous potentially fractious inter-Allied Conferences at the height of the war, including Casablanca (January1943), Quebec (August 1943), Cairo (November 1943), Teheran (November 1943), Quebec (September 1944), and Yalta (1944). These were often tricky affairs in which he had to deal with the undoubted tensions that existed between Churchill and the Soviet leader Stalin. The reality of the political situation meant that Roosevelt had to compromise on several aspects of the Atlantic Charter's proposals for the postwar world.

His chief concern was to ensure that worldwide opinion was supportive of the Allies, who were portrayed as the defenders of democracy and in this he succeeded, although he was never able to engineer the end of British colonialism that he desired, nor reach an accommodation with the Soviet Union. Yet for all his towering and successful efforts on behalf of the Allied cause during the war years, Roosevelt did not live to see the defeat of the Axis powers. He died on 12 April 1945, just a few months before the end of the fighting.

war against the United States four days later. Roosevelt immediately instigated two key policies. First, there would obviously be a war on two fronts, in the Pacific and Europe, but Germany was to be defeated first.

Second the United States' vast industrial base and natural resources would become the "arsenal of democracy"—by fueling the war efforts of the other Allies.

Roosevelt was a hugely popular

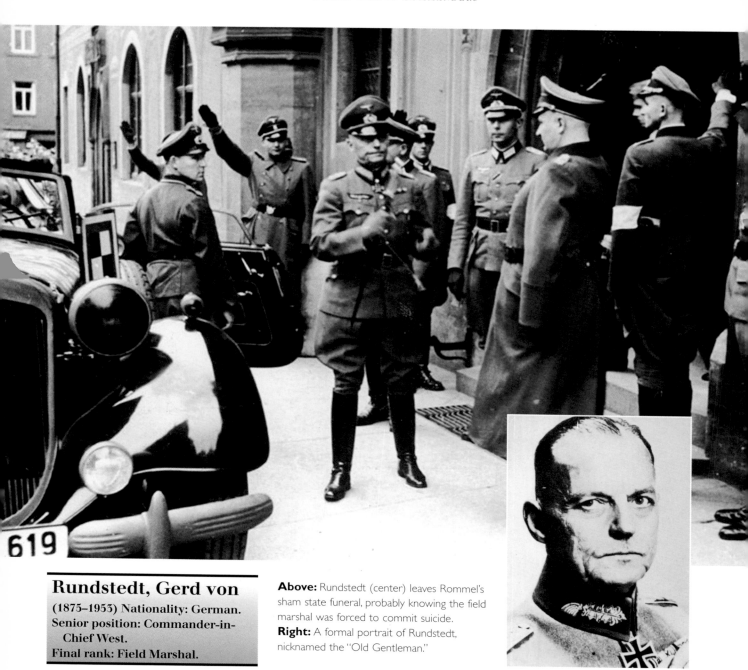

619

Rundstedt, Gerd von

**(1875–1953) Nationality: German.
Senior position: Commander-in-
Chief West.
Final rank: Field Marshal.**

Above: Rundstedt (center) leaves Rommel's sham state funeral, probably knowing the field marshal was forced to commit suicide.
Right: A formal portrait of Rundstedt, nicknamed the "Old Gentleman."

Rundstedt was born into the Prussian aristocracy and became a career soldier who briefly served on the Western Front in 1914 before being wounded. After recovering he held a number of staff posts and remained in

Below: Rundstedt was captured by the Allies in May 1945 and was held in an English prison for three years.

the service during the interwar years, but went into retirement in October 1938. Despite his dislike for Hitler, a view he expressed only in private, he returned at the beginning of May 1939 and was ordered to plan the invasion of Poland. This task was rapidly completed and Rundstedt took charge of Army Group South for the actual invasion in September. He was next

given charge of Army Group A, which spearheaded the invasion of France and the Low Countries in May the following year, its armor making the decisive breakthrough at Sedan.

Rundstedt was promoted to the rank of field marshal in July even though his controversial decision to halt attacks against the Dunkirk perimeter and leave the reduction

work to the *Luftwaffe* greatly facilitated the escape of the British Expeditionary Force. Nevertheless, after a spell as commander-in-chief in the west, he transferred to the east in March 1941 and then led Army Group South in the invasion of the Ukraine during the opening stagers of Operation Barbarossa. Rundstedt was sacked by Hitler in early December after he had withdrawn without seeking permission in the face of fierce attacks by the Red Army. However, Hitler learned that the field marshal had suffered a heart attack during the fighting and sent him a large financial gift, much to his embarrassment.

Rundstedt returned to serve as commander in the west in March 1942, with responsibility for defending Fortress Europe, but was caught napping by the June 1944 D-Day landings with his troops out of position. He was dismissed for a second time in July. Rundstedt never really lost Hitler's admiration and confidence so he was again recalled in September to mastermind the ultimately unsuccessful Ardennes Offensive and the defense of the Rhineland. This was his swansong, and he was dismissed for good in March 1945. He was subsequently held in captivity by the British for three years.

Left: Rundstedt was drawn from the Prussian aristocracy and had old-style attributes—he was loyal and honest, and displayed great calm when events turned for the worst.

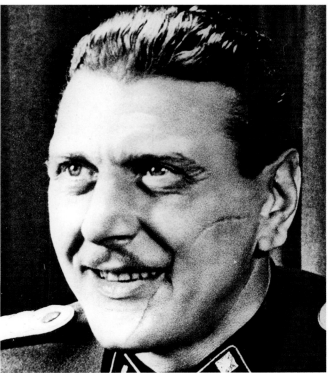

Sikorski, Wladyslaw

(1881–1943) Nationality: Polish.
Senior position: Commander-in-Chief Free Polish
  Forces.
Final rank: General.

Skorzeny, Otto

(1908–1975) Nationality: German.
Senior position: Commander 150th Panzer Brigade.
Final rank: Lieutenant-Colonel.

Sikorski did not take part in the defense of his homeland in 1939 but soon became head of the government in exile and the Free Polish Forces. These were initially based in France and by the next year comprised some 100,000 men. He transferred to Britain in 1940, brokered an alliance with the Russians, but died in an air crash

Skorzeny was a leading exponent of unconventional operations and first came to prominence when he and a small force rescued Mussolini from captivity in September 1943. In 1944 he successfully prevented Hungary from negotiating an armistice with Russia, and led a largely unsuccessfully deception brigade in the Battle of the Bulge.

Above: Sikorski died while returning from a visit to Polish troops training in Iraq.

Above: Skorzeny, who was intensely loyal to Hitler, stood trial at Nuremberg but was acquitted of war crimes.

Slim, William

**(1891–1971) Nationality: British.
Senior position: Commander-in-
 Chief Allied Land Forces
 Southeast Asia.
Final rank: General.**

In 1940 Slim took command of a division of Indian troops and led them against the Italians at the Battle of Gallabat in the Sudan, where he was later wounded. He recovered and commanded the same unit during military operations in Iraq the following year. In mid-1941 he participated in the occupation of Vichy French Syria and then invaded Iran to quell an imminent revolt that was being encouraged by Nazi agents. The campaign ended when Slim entered Teheran, the capital.

He was sent out to the Far East to take charge of Burma I Corps in March 1942. The situation was deteriorating fast as the British and local troops were in the middle of a morale-sapping retreat over hundreds of miles of difficult terrain. Many of them did eventually escape capture or death at the hands of the Japanese invaders and reached India, but they were in no position to launch counter-attacks. Slim was ordered to take over another corps and set about revitalizing it as a fighting force. His qualities were fully recognized in the latter part of 1943, when he was given command of the Fourteenth Army, which had been ordered to retake Burma despite being somewhat starved of supplies for the remainder of the war.

Slim moved to block a Japanese thrust into the Arakan region of Burma in February 1944 and then the Japanese launched a major offensive towards the border towns of Imphal and Kohima in March. This was eventually beaten off by July and the Japanese were forced into a major withdrawal that cost them thousands of troops. Slim followed them methodically and retook Mandalay at the end of March 1945. He then raced south to take the capital, Rangoon, unopposed, in May. During the final months his command was engaged in mopping-up operations across the Far East, including Malaya and Indonesia.

Below: Slim (right) holds an impromptu discussion with Mountbatten (left) during the Burma campaign.

Smith, Holland

(1882–1867) Nationality: American.
Senior position: Commander Fleet Marine Force
Pacific.
Final rank: General.

Smith was the leading exponent of amphibious warfare in the Pacific and took part in virtually all of the campaign's major assaults. As the commander of V Amphibious Corps, he led his marines in the Aleutians, the Gilberts, the Marshalls, and in the Marianas, as well as holding even more senior rank for Iwo Jima and Okinawa.

Above: Smith (right) congratulates the commander of the US 3rd Marine Division for its part in taking Iwo Jima, March 1945.

Smith, Walter Bedell

(1895–1961) Nationality: American.
Senior position: Chief-of-Staff to Allied Supreme
Commander.
Final rank: General.

Smith was made secretary of the US Joint Chiefs-of-Staff and US secretary of the Anglo-American Combined Chiefs-of-Staff in December 1941. He became Eisenhower's chief-of-staff in 1942. He also oversaw the Italian armistice in 1943 and arranged the German surrender in the west in May 1945.

Above: Smith proved an outstanding chief-of-staff to Eisenhower but was also harsh, quick-tempered, and abrupt.

Smuts, Jan

(1870–1950) Nationality: South African.
Senior position: Prime Minister.
Final rank: Field Marshal.

Smuts was a soldier-statesman who had held senior positions in the British War Cabinet and in the field during the East African campaign in World War I. On the eve of World War II he was deputy prime minister in a coalition government formed from his own Union Party and the National Party, but it fell apart once the hostilities had begun with the invasion of Poland in September 1939. The key issue was over supporting Britain. The National Party was largely opposed, favoring an isolationist policy. Smuts, who was pro-intervention, won the fraught debate. The incumbent prime minister resigned and Smuts became the new head of government, a position he had previously held from 1919 to 1924.

Below: Smuts (right) confers with various officers in North Africa, including Tedder (left), commander of the Middle East Air Force.

Smuts took on further responsibilities for running his country's war effort over the following months and by 1940 was head of its armed forces. He was also highly supportive of Churchill—the two became close friends—and his policies throughout the conflict, and became involved in various key conferences, including attending the San Francisco Conference to compose the United Nations Charter in 1945. He was made an honorary field marshal in the British Army in 1941 but preferred to use his old rank of general. He remained in office until 1948.

Left: Smuts had fought against the British in the Second Anglo-Boer War but later became a staunch supporter of his former enemy.

Below: Smuts on a tour of inspection of South African troops in the Western Desert.

Somerville, James

(1882–1949) Nationality: British.
Senior position: Commander-in-Chief Eastern Fleet.
Final rank: Admiral.

Spaatz, Carl

(1891–1974) Nationality: American.
Senior position: Commander US Army Air Forces
**   Europe and Pacific.**
Final rank: General.

Somerville commanded Force H, the Gibraltar-based fleet that attacked the French naval bases at Oran and Mers-el-Kebir in July 1940, and he was involved in the sinking of the *Bismarck* in 1941. He was the senior British naval commander in the Far East between 1942 and 1944 and ended the war as head of the British naval delegation in Washington.

Spatz held a number of senior air force positions throughout the war and made his combat debut as commander of the Eighth Army Air Force based in England. Thereafter he served in North Africa before returning to England as head of the US air forces in Europe. He transferred to the Pacific in March 1945 to occupy a similar position.

Above: Somerville was actually invalided out of the navy in 1939 but returned to service the following year.

Above: Spaatz directed the final stages of the strategic bomber offensive against Japan, including the use of two atomic bombs.

Speer, Albert
(1905–1981) Nationality: German.
Senior position: Minister of
Armaments and Munitions.

Speer, an architect by training, was attracted to the Nazi Party but did not become a fully paid up member until 1932. He went further by also joining the SS and his first major appointment was to organize the Nuremburg Rally of 1934. When war came, he was given the task of overseeing the building of armaments factories and various military installations. His big break came in February 1942 when the head of the Organization Todt died in a plane crash. Speer was placed in charge of this vast conglomerate that ultimately used not only German and foreign workers on construction and industrial production projects but also forced labor.

He revitalized the organization and made it more efficient, and the next year was given total control over the war economy. Despite many organizational problems and the ever-growing Allied strategic bomber offensive, he succeeded in tripling armaments production between 1942 and 1944 and thus undoubtedly

Above: Speer (at Hitler's left) pictured when he was head of the Organization Todt, a position he gained in early 1942.

prolonged the war. At the very end of the war Speer held the position of economy minister for seven days until surrendering to the Allies. He was tried at Nuremburg, where he distanced himself from Hitler but did accept collective responsibility for the regime's crimes. He was sentenced to twenty years' imprisonment for the use of forced labor and served the full term.

Sperrle, Hugo

(1885–1953) Nationality: German.
Senior position: Commander Luftflotte III.
Final rank: Field Marshal.

Sperrle led the Condor Legion for part of the Spanish Civil War and was given command of the *Luftwaffe*'s *Luftflotte III* (Air Fleet III) in 1939. This supported the *Blitzkriegs* across Europe and played a major part in the Battle of Britain, in which it suffered heavy losses. Sperrle remained in France but was dismissed for incompetence in August 1944.

Above: Sperrle commanded *Luftflotte III* during the Battle of Britain and remained in Western Europe thereafter.

Spruance, Raymond

(1886–1969) Nationality: American.
Senior position: Commander 5th Fleet.
Final rank: Vice-Admiral.

Spruance, probably the best field commander in the US Navy during the war, started the conflict at Midway as the leader of a cruiser squadron, but was promoted to take command of Task Force 16 in June 1942 to oppose any Japanese attempts to take the strategically important island in the Central Pacific. TF16 was built around two

Left: A formal portrait of Admiral Spruance.

Above: Spruance (left) chats with Nimitz (center), 8 April 1944.

carriers, but when that of their commander, *Yorktown*, was put out of action shortly after the Battle of Midway began, Spruance took direct control of the complex action. He inflicted a severe defeat on the Japanese, sinking four valuable carriers, and shortly afterwards was made Nimitz's chief-of-staff. He became involved in strategic planning. However, he returned to front-line service in August 1943 when he was given charge of a fleet, which operated in the Central Pacific Area. His first task was to take part in the bloody capture of the Gilbert Islands in November, and he went on to capture the Marshall Islands in January 1944.

The next month saw Spruance's fleet take part in operations against the Truk in the Caroline Islands. His greatest challenge took place later in the year when he was involved in the landings on Saipan, one of the Mariana Islands. The invasion began on 10 June and eight days later Spruance's fleet, which was protecting the amphibious assault forces, became embroiled in a decisive two-day fight with a major Japanese task force. The Battle of the Philippine Sea, which also became known to the US naval aviators as the "Great Marianas Turkey Shoot," saw Spruance destroy virtually all of what remained of Japan's once mighty naval aviation arm. Even so, some claimed that he could have gone further and annihilated his opponents.

His next task was to participate in the invasion of Iwo Jima in early 1945 and, as the war moved ever nearer to Japan's home islands, launch carrier raids on Tokyo. His last effort was to plan what proved to be the unnecessary invasion of Japan. Spruance was cautious in action but cool-headed, and he pioneered some of the naval techniques that made the US island-hopping campaign across the Pacific to Japan both viable and ultimately successful.

Stalin, Joseph

(1879–1953) Nationality: Georgian.
Senior position: Soviet Leader.

Stalin was unique among the senior political figures in the Allied camp in that he also effectively headed the Soviet Union's high command for the entire war. Despite having no military experience whatsoever—he had been declared medically unfit to fight in World War I—he named himself

Above: Stalin looks on as the Non-Aggression Pact with Germany is signed, 23 August 1939.

Right: Stalin (third from right) attends an Allied conference at the end of the war.

commander-in-chief of the armed forces. This was in part because he suspected that Red Army officers in particular were disloyal to him personally; he had initiated a purge of those he suspected of holding such views in 1937.

As the war clouds gathered over Europe, he was acutely aware that the Soviet Union was not ready for war and so agreed a non-aggression pact with Germany in 1939. This gave him the opportunity to occupy the eastern

Below: The "Big Three"—Stalin, Roosevelt, and Churchill—attending the Tehran conference in 1943.

half of Poland the following month, to create a buffer zone between the Soviet Union proper and its likely future enemy. In 1939–1940 Stalin also embarked on a war with Finland that went badly wrong but did finally push the Russo-Finnish border away from Leningrad. In June 1940 his forces were able to occupy the Baltic States to create another buffer zone. Stalin also ended his military purges within the Soviet Union and redirected his efforts towards the newly conquered states.

Events elsewhere caught Stalin by surprise, especially the rapid fall of France in 1940. He now recognized

that a war with Nazi Germany would take place sooner than he anticipated, although he still clung to the view that Hitler would not break their non-aggression pact for some time. Despite having been informed of an imminent invasion, he prevented the mobilization of the Red Army in mid-June 1941, so that it was ill-prepared to meet the *Blitzkrieg* that opened on the 22nd. Over the next few days his forces suffered horrendous losses of both men and equipment, and he came close to mental collapse.

Stalin recovered his nerve and exhorted the Russian people to stiffen the resistance. By the end of the

Above: Stalin photographed in the company of the recently elevated Truman and Churchill, probably at the Potsdam Conference in July 1945.

month he had formed a committee of defense and on 10 July named himself supreme commander. The German advance was halted outside Moscow in December and Stalin now urged his commanders to counterattack, despite the parlous state of the Red Army. The attacks over the next six months failed with heavy losses but they did teach Stalin some invaluable lessons that he would put to good use when ordering future offensives.

Even as the Red Army was rebuilding, Stalin was galvanizing the wider nation for the battles to come. Industry was relocated to safer areas and the Russian people were encouraged to ever greater efforts, to play their part in the defense of the motherland. The fight-back came, perhaps not surprisingly, at Stalingrad, the city that he could not allow to fall in German hands. It was fully secured by the end of January 1943, by which time the Soviet Union's production of both tanks and aircraft had far outstripped that of Germany.

Stalin still ran the war—he worked up to fourteen hours a day—but he gradually came to rely on, if not entirely trust, a rising group of young senior commanders. He was not afraid of shouting them down or humiliating them in public but he was equally willing to shower them with gifts and awards if they performed well. The next key moment came in mid-1943, when the Red Army won the Battle of Kursk. This huge engagement destroyed Germany's strategic military reserve and ensured that henceforth it would be in retreat and could only fight defensive actions.

Henceforth Stalin became increasingly pre-occupied with other matters, particularly the nature of the postwar world in Europe. He wanted to bring Poland under the Soviet umbrella after Germany had been defeated, but the western Allies wanted to see the creation of a free, democratic country. A decision of sorts was made at Yalta in early 1945. The western Allies agreed to spheres of influence in Europe, which left the Soviet Union in control of its eastern and much of central zones. The western Allies thought these would be temporary; Stalin saw no reason why the arrangement could not be permanent.

The war was won the following May, and Stalin's role in bringing about Germany's defeat is complex. The Soviet Union bore the overwhelming brunt of the war in eastern Europe from 1941 onwards and without his iron will, ruthlessness, and determination it seems likely that the USSR would have collapsed. Yet victory was bought at a high price. Stalin made several disastrous military decisions that cost an untold number of military lives, and he was equally willing to use violence against his own or subject peoples. He did create a cult of personality around himself that ensured him widespread popularity, and on the back of this remained the unchallenged leader until his death.

Stark, Harold
(1880–1972) Nationality: American.
Senior position: Commander US Naval Forces Europe.
Final rank: Admiral.

Stark was commander of naval operations in 1939 and did much to prepare the US Navy for war. He put its warships on high alert just before the Pearl Harbor attack but failed to give sufficient warning to its base commander. Stark was given the largely diplomatic but nevertheless important position of head of naval forces in Europe in early 1942.

Above: Stark's career was blighted because he held the US Navy's highest post at the time of Pearl Harbor.

Stilwell, Joseph

**(1883–1946) Nationality: American.
Senior position: Chinese Nationalist
Chief-of-Staff.
Final rank: General.**

Stilwell was something of an expert on the Far East, having been the military attaché at the US embassy in Beijing from 1932 to 1939. In 1941 he was ordered by the War Department to take command of all the US forces in the Burma, China, and India region and also to improve the armed forces of the Chinese Nationalists, chiefly by insuring that the US aid being sent to them was used properly. By early 1942 Stilwell was not only directing the operations of two Chinese armies in northern Burma but he was also

Above: Stilwell (center, facing camera) talks to members of Merrill's Marauders during the push on Myitkyina, Burma, in 1944.

acting as chief -of-staff to the Nationalist leader, Chiang Kai-shek. They had a somewhat difficult relationship.

In late summer 1943 the Allies reorganized their command structure into the Southeast Asia Zone and

Stilwell was appointed its deputy commander under Mountbatten. He also continued to exercise field command and from late 1943 until August 1944 was involved in operations to capture the important town of Myitkyina in Burma. There were US-led moves to make Stilwell the commander of all Chinese Nationalist forces but Chiang Kai-shek ordered that he be recalled in October. His last role was as commander of the Tenth Army on Okinawa.

Left: Stilwell takes time out to clean his Thompson submachine gun during a lull in the action, May 1942.
Below: The general (left) talks to Brigadier General Frank Merrill, commander of the Marauders.

Student, Kurt

(1890–1978) Nationality: German.
Senior position: Commander Army Group G.
Final rank: General.

Takagi, Takeo

(1892–1944) Nationality: Japanese.
Senior position: Commander Sixth Submarine Fleet.
Final rank: Vice-Admiral.

Formerly a World War I aviator, Student joined the *Luftwaffe* in 1934 and was chosen to develop its paratrooper and glider arms. They both played a significant part in the invasion of France and the Low Countries in 1940 but were badly mauled on Crete the next year. Student served for the remainder of the war, ending it in command of an army group.

Above: German paratroopers, part of the elite force Student helped establish, exit a Junkers Ju 52 transport.

Takagi was a commander of the Imperial Japanese Navy's support forces and was present at most of the early battles of the war in the Pacific, including the Battles of the Java Sea and Midway in February and June 1942. He was posted to Saipan to take charge of a submarine fleet in 1943 but was killed during the battle for the island in 1944.

Above: Takagi won tactical victories over the US Navy at the Battles of the Java and the Coral Seas in 1942.

Tedder, Arthur

(1890–1967) Nationality: British.
Senior position: Deputy Supreme Commander Allied
    Expeditionary Force.
Final rank: Air Marshal.

Tedder was one of the best air officers of the war and was first noticed when he was made commander-in-chief of Britain's Middle East Air Force in 1941. He repeatedly stressed the need to gain air superiority in the theater but his cynicism almost resulted in Churchill dismissing him. Nevertheless, his view was borne out and the air force's superiority over its *Luftwaffe* opponents was a major factor

Below: Tedder (to Eisenhower's right) attends a meeting of senior figures in the Supreme Headquarters Allied Expeditionary Force before D-Bay.

Tanaka, Raizo

(1892–1969) Nationality: Japanese.
Senior position: Task Force commander.
Final rank: Rear-Admiral.

Tanaka was involved in virtually every major surface action in the Pacific in the first eighteen months of the war. He commanded the Midway Occupation Force's transport group during 1942 and then participated in actions off the Solomons. Tanaka was criticized for failing to deliver supplies to the garrison on Guadalcanal and was recalled the next year.

Above: Tanaka was considered by the US Navy to be Japan's best commander of destroyers.

in bringing about victory at the Second Battle of El Alamein in late 1942. His squadrons also operated what became known as "Tedder's Carpet," a tactic in which enemy positions were repeatedly bombed and strafed immediately before the attacking advanced ground units.

Tedder became Eisenhower's army and air force deputy at the 1943 Casablanca Conference and was tasked with coordinating these forces for the invasions of Sicily in July and the Italian mainland in September. Back in England in 1944 he was not only Eisenhower's deputy but also supreme air commander, the latter role requiring him to identify the correct strategy for the deployment of both fighter and bomber units during the buildup to the Normandy landings. He was then put in charge of the Allied Tactical Air Force over northwest Europe and, as Eisenhower's representative, was Allied signatory to the surrender document for the German forces in the west in May 1945.

Terauchi, Hisaichi

(1879–1946) Nationality: Japanese.
Senior position: Commander Southern Army.
Final rank: Field Marshal.

Terauchi was made head of an army in late 1941 and he occupied all the US, British, and Dutch possessions in his area of operations. He ordered the construction of the Burma Road during 1942, a project that cost the lives of some 50,000 Allied prisoners. He suffered a stroke in September 1945 and formally surrendered only during November.

Above: Terauchi was one of the most highly regarded Japanese officers, renowned for his magnanimous personality.

Tito, Josip Broz

(1892–1980) Nationality: Yugoslavian.
Senior position' Yugoslavian Communist Resistance
    Leader.
Final rank: Marshal.

Tito (born Josip Broz, the codename Tito later being adopted as surname) was a communist of long standing, and was one of the leading figures in the Yugoslavian resistance movement after the German invasion of April 1941. He began by mounting pinprick sabotage attacks in July but these escalated into a major campaign in Serbia later the same year. Tito's guerrillas increasingly clashed with the Chetniks, a right-wing resistance group that collaborated with the invaders, but were able to inflict severe casualties on them. However, Tito was eventually driven out of Serbia in the first of seven major anti-partisan sweeps by the Germans, some of which came close to

Below: Tito pictured studying maps and documents in one of his many headquarters in mountainous Yugoslavia.

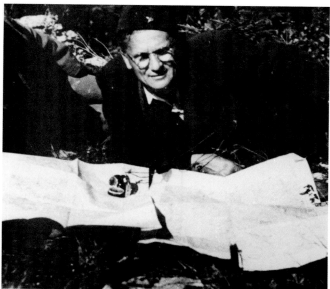

Timoshenko, Semyon

(1895–1970) Nationality: Russian.
Senior position: Marshal of the Soviet Union.
Final rank: Field Marshal.

Timoshenko was given command of the Western Front in June 1941 and narrowly avoided encirclement at Smolensk, but recovered to delay the enemy advance on Moscow. He was then given the Southwest Front but failed to halt further German pushes. After failure of an offensive on Kharkov in 1942, he was transferred to the quieter Northwest Front.

Above: Timoshenko's final acts of the war were to capture Vienna on 13 April 1945 and then link up with US forces at Linz on 6 May.

Above: Tito (right) was leader of one of the first anti-fascist military formations in Europe.

crushing the guerrillas entirely and killing or capturing him.

As Tito bore the burden of the Yugoslavian resistance movement, the initially reluctant western Allies slowly began to channel weapons and equipment to his forces from 1942, a period when the Chetniks' collaboration was becoming ever more evident.

His position became even stronger after Italy left the war in September 1943, by which time he had some 250,000 men and women under arms. Confirmation of his position came in May 1944 when the Yugoslavian government-in-exile removed the Chetniks' leader and began negotiating with Tito. His forces recaptured

Belgrade in October 1944 and had liberated most of the country by the war's end. His communist party won the first elections.

Togo, Shigenori
(1882–1950) Nationality: Japanese.
Senior position: Foreign Minister.

A career diplomat after abandoning his position as a university teacher, Togo was, unlike many of those who moved in his country's political and military circles, both anti-war and opposed to militarism. Renowned for being both insightful and forthright, in the interwar years he undertook a number of overseas postings, including stints as ambassador to both Germany and then the Soviet Union. He twice served as foreign minister, and argued for any early peace with the United States. He resigned for the first time over matters of policy in September 1943.

Togo remained on the sidelines for the next several months but returned to the same position in April 1945, but only on the understanding that his role would be to seek peace with the Allies. He finally resigned from the government in August 1945, after the surrender terms had been agreed, but was arrested in 1946. He was tried, convicted of committing "crimes of conspiracy against peace," and give a twenty-year prison term. He died before completing the sentence.

Left: Togo had a brief career as a university teacher before embarking on a career as a diplomat in 1912. His first major overseas posting came in 1937, when he was made Japan's ambassador to Germany.

Tojo, Hideki

**(1884–1948) Nationality: Japanese.
Senior position: Prime
    Minister/War Minister.
Final rank: General.**

The son of a general, Tojo was a career army officer with political ambitions. He was not regarded as particularly bright but was hard-working and made a decent staff officer. An arch nationalist, he was also leader of the *Toseiha*, an extremist military group that wanted the army to have a more prominent role in Japan's political life, and he also fully supported Japan's territorial ambitions in the Pacific and China. He gradually rose in seniority, becoming the chief-of-staff of the Kwantung Army in China during 1937 and then deputy war minister a mere year later.

He served as war minister between 1940 and 1941 and was made prime minister in October of the latter year. Tojo now moved to dominate the government by holding a number of key posts, including that of chief-of-staff from early 1944, but he resigned in July that year as the war news worsened. Taken prisoner by the Allies after a failed suicide bid with a pistol, he was later put on trial. He was found guilty on several counts, including "ordering, authorizing and permitting atrocities," and hanged.

Left: Tojo was Japan's political and military leader during the war and was nicknamed "Kamisori" (Razor) for his strictness and fascination with minor details.

Toyoda, Soemu

(1885–1957) Nationality: Japanese.
Senior position: Commander-in-
Chief Combined Fleet.
Final rank: Admiral.

Toyodo took command of the main battle fleet in early 1943 and sought a decisive battle with his US opponents, but this resulted in catastrophic defeats at the Battles of the Philippine Sea and Leyte Gulf in June and October 1944. His last major act was to send the huge battleship *Yamato* on a pointless suicide mission to Okinawa in April 1945.

Left: Toyodo wished to continue the war even when Japan's defeat was inevitable. He stood trial for war crimes but was acquitted.

Truman, Harry

(1884–1972) Nationality: American.
Senior position: President.

Truman, a World War I veteran and former county judge, was serving as a Democratic senator for Missouri at the beginning of US involvement in World War II. He was detailed to chair a special committee looking into rumors of the misuse of funds and the illegal allocation of contracts by members of the National Defense Program. Many opposed the creation of the committee but it had support in high places and Truman was able to get to work. He handled what was a

delicate mission with extreme tact, saving the administration millions of dollars and minimizing any fall-out from the few scandals he uncovered. The investigative board under his leadership simply became known as the "Truman Committee."

His good work led to Truman being adopted as Roosevelt's vice-president in 1944 and took over the

Above: Truman gives a press conference in the White House's oval office. As the war had only a few months to run when he became president, he concentrated on shaping the peace.

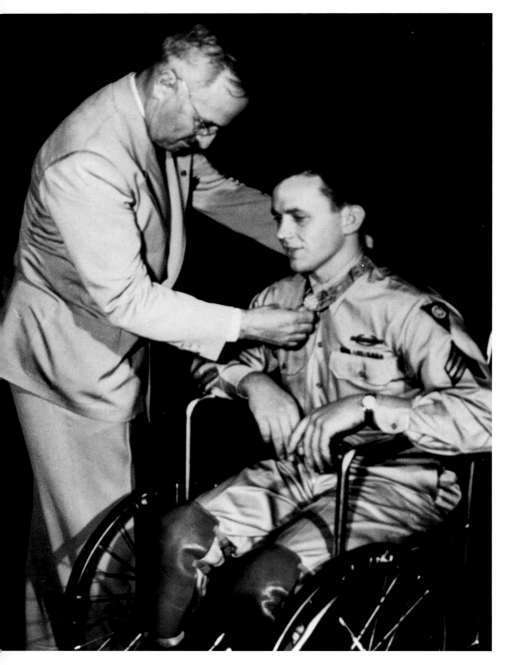

top job after the latter's death on 12 April 1945. At this point the war against Germany was all but over and a more pressing problem there was the failing relationship with the Soviet Union and the shaping of postwar Europe. However, the Pacific campaign had several more months to run at the very least and the US military were drawing up plans to invade the Japan's home islands, an unappetizing prospect that most felt would lead to horrendous civilian and military casualties.

Truman continued to pursue many of Roosevelt's policies, not least at the San Francisco Conference in late April, at which the outline of the United Nations Charter was revealed. He also tried to get reassurances from an increasingly stubborn Stalin regarding the postwar fate of Poland but the latter refused to compromise and proved especially difficult at the Potsdam Conference in July-August 1945. Returning home from this meeting, Truman decided to use the atomic bomb to bring about Japan's immediate surrender and perhaps, as some have suggested, send out a warning to Stalin. Whatever the truth of the matter Japan surrendered on 14 August after atomic bombs had been dropped on Hiroshima and Nagasaki. Truman served another seven years as president.

Left: Truman presents the Medal of Honor to badly injured US Army Sergeant Ralph G. Keppel.

Turner, Richmond

(1885–1961) Nationality: American.
Senior position: Commander
Amphibious Forces Pacific.
Final rank: Admiral.

Turner was made commander of an amphibious force in the Pacific in 1942 and his first job was to put marines ashore on Guadalcanal. After a bout of malaria, he oversaw landings on New Georgia and the Gilbert Islands. Thereafter he worked in the Central Pacific Area and played an important part in virtually every major amphibious operation until 1945.

Right: Turner (center) celebrates the fall of Iwo Jima with Marine commanders Harry Schmidt (left) and Holland Smith, March 1945.

Twining, Nathan

(1897–1982) Nationality: American.
Senior position: Commander 15th
Air Force.
Final rank: General .

Twining was a superb exponent of strategic bombing. Between 1942 and 1943 he was chief-of-staff to the commander in the South Pacific Area and in the latter year took over the 13th Army Air Force, which was operating over Guadalcanal. Next he transferred to Italy to lead the 15th Army Air Force and ended the war directing bombing raids on Japan.

Above: Twining (right) with army commanders Harmon (center) and Patch, 1943.

Udet, Ernst

(1896–1941) Nationality: German.
Senior position: Commander Office of Air Armament.
Final rank: Colonel-General.

Ushijima, Mitsuru

(1887–1945) Nationality: Japanese.
Senior position: Commander Thirty-second Army.
Final rank: Lieutenant-General.

Udet earned his credentials in World War I and in 1936 was made head of the *Luftwaffe*'s Technical Office. Three years later he took over the Office of Air Armament but proved inadequate. Work pressure led him to commit suicide, although the authorities ascribed his death to an air crash.

Ushijima was commandant of the Japanese Military Academy until 1942 and then served on Iwo Jima and Okinawa, where he commanded the army-sized garrison that opposed the US landings in 1945. A determined defense could not save the island, and he committed ritual suicide as defeat beckoned..

Above: Udet poses by a glider at the time of the Berlin Olympic Games of 1936.

Above: Ushijima conducted a brilliant if bloody and ultimately unsuccessful defense of Okinawa in April-June 1945.

Vandegrift, Alexander
(1887–1973) Nationality: American.
Senior position: Commandant-General Marine Corps.
Final rank: Lieutenant-General.

Vatutin, Nikolai
(1901–1944) Nationality: Russian.
Senior position: Commander Southwest Front.
Final rank: General.

Vandegrift commanded the 1st Marine Division from early 1942 and played a pivotal role in the assault on Guadalcanal later the same year. He was then given the I Marine Amphibious Corps in mid-1943, which took part in the Bougainville landings, and was made head of the entire Marine Corps in 1944.

Above: Vandegrift conducted the first successful US amphibious assault of the war—that against Guadalcanal.

Vatutin was the Soviet Union's head of General Staff operations but proved his worth as a commander during the defense of Moscow in 1941 and at Stalingrad. His forces played a decisive role at Kursk in 1943 and then recaptured Kiev. He was fatally wounded when his car was ambushed, possibly by Ukrainian nationalist partisans, early the next year.

Above: Vatutin was a career soldier, one who proved to be an excellent army group commander.

Vian, Philip

(1894–1968) Nationality: British.
Senior position: Commander Eastern Fleet's Carrier
    Squadron.
Final rank: Admiral.

Vietinghoff, Heinrich

(1887–1952) Nationality: German.
Senior position: Commander-in-Chief Italy.
Final rank: General.

Vian made his reputation during operations off Norway and subsequently transferred to the Mediterranean, leading an aircraft carrier force during the 1943 Salerno landings in Italy. He later commanded the Eastern Task Force during the Normandy landings and was then sent to the Pacific, where he participated in the fight for Okinawa.

Above: Vian was one of the most dashing and successful naval commanders of the war, taking part in many major operations.

Vietinghoff commanded a German tank division during the Polish invasion of 1939, led a corps during the 1940 *Blitzkrieg* on Western Europe, and then took over an army on the Eastern Front. He transferred to Italy in mid-1943 and became commander there in 1945, when he negotiated with the Allies to bring about his forces' surrender.

Above: Vietinghoff secretly contacted the Allies to bring about the surrender of German forces in Italy some six days before elsewhere in Europe.

Vlasov, Andrei

(1900–1946) Nationality; Russian.
Senior position: Commander Second Shock Army.
Final rank: Lieutenant-General.

Voroshilov, Kliment

(1881–1969) Nationality: Russian.
Senior position: Deputy Chairman State Defense
**   Committee.**
Final rank: Marshal.

Vlasov was a Russian general of some note but was profoundly anti-Soviet. Captured by the Germans in 1942, he was used as a propaganda tool and given command of the so-called Russian Liberation Army. He surrendered to US forces in 1945 but was handed over to the Soviet authorities and hanged as a traitor.

Above: Vlasov's attempts to recruit Russian prisoners in Germany to fight against the Soviet Union were hampered by Hitler's doubts.

Voroshilov was a senior figure in the Soviet Union's military-political hierarchy and became a member of the general headquarters in mid-1941. But his failure to halt the German drive on Leningrad ended his active field command. He spent the remainder of the war in various staff positions and attending several inter-Allied conferences.

Above: Voroshilov held several staff positions during the war and would eventually become the Soviet Union's president.

Wavell, Archibald
(1883–1950) Nationality: British.
Senior position: Commander-in-Chief Middle East.
Final rank: Field Marshal.

Wavell, who had served in World War I, was made Britain's overall commander in the Middle East and North Africa in July 1939, and within months his small Western Desert Force in Egypt was attacked by much larger Italian forces from neighboring Cyrenaica. He replied with a fast-moving armored counterthrust that pushed the invaders back and took some 100,000 prisoners in a matter of weeks. He then campaigned with equal success in East Africa, forcing the Italians there to surrender in early April 1941.

A sizeable part of his command had by this stage of the war been sent to Greece and those remaining troops in North Africa were soon outmaneuvered by Rommel and the *Afrika Korps*. Wavell, who was disliked by Churchill, was transferred to India at the latter's insistence, becoming the Allied supreme commander, but he resigned in February 1942. He returned to action in December but failure in the Arakan in Burma again attracted Churchill's ire and Wavell was moved sideways to take up the purely political post of viceroy of India.

Above: Wavell, seen here inspecting Chindits in Burma, previously saw service in the Second Anglo-Boer War and World War I, during which he lost an eye.

Wedemeyer, Albert

(1897–1990) Nationality: American.
Senior position: Chinese
Nationalists' Chief-of-Staff.
Final rank: Major-General.

Wedemeyer held a number of US staff positions from 1941 but in 1943 he was made US deputy chief-of-staff for the Southeast Asia Command, serving under Britain's Lord Louis Mountbatten in India. Wedemeyer became the chief-of-staff to Chinese Nationalist leader Chiang Kai-shek in September 1944 and held the position until the war's end.

Below: Wedermeyer, commander of US Army Air Forces in China, attends a conference with several US and Chinese officers.

Weygand, Maxime

(1867–1965) Nationality:
French/Belgian
Senior position: Supreme Allied
Commander France.
Final rank: General.

Weygand, who was stationed in the Middle East, was ordered back to France as Allied commander-in-chief during May 1940 but failed to halt the German *Blitzkrieg* and successfully argued for the armistice signed in June. He was then sent to command troops in North Africa but was removed from his post at German insistence in 1941. The latter held him prisoner between 1942 and 1945.

Right: Although he served in the Vichy French government, Weygand appears to have been irreconcilably anti-Nazi.

Wilson, Henry

(1881–1964) Nationality: British.
Senior position: Supreme Allied Commander
  Mediterranean.
Final rank: Field Marshal.

Wingate, Orde

(1903–1944) Nationality: British
Senior position: Commander Chindits
Final rank: Major-General

Wilson spent the greater part of the war overseeing British affairs in the Mediterranean and, despite a succession of major set-backs, Churchill never lost confidence in him. He was made head of Allied forces in the Mediterranean in 1944 and was then sent to the United States as leader of the British Joint Staff Mission.

Above: Wilson shown with the shoulder patch of the Allied Forces Headquarters, the first Allied inter-service headquarters formed in August 1942.

Wingate was a leading exponent of unconventional warfare and had cut his teeth with the British-Israeli Special Night Squads that combated Arab nationalists in Palestine in the late 1930s. After the outbreak of World War II, he led the so-called Gideon Force during successful hit-and-run operations against the Italians in Ethiopia during

Above: Wingate (center) poses with some of his Chindit officers, including Major Michael "Mad Mike" Calvert (left).

late 1940. He entered Addis Abada in triumph, but his career then stalled when he was given a desk job. He subsequently suffered from depression, and attempted suicide when struck down by a bout of malaria.

Salvation came when he transferred to India to form Long Range Penetration Groups. Better known as the Chindits, these brigade-sized units first went into action in February 1943 and, despite the heavy losses suffered on this first operation, it made Wingate a national hero and showed that British forces could fight the Japanese on equal terms in the jungle. A second, more ambitious mission involving six brigades began in February 1944 but Wingate was killed in a jungle air crash the following month.

Below: Wingate chats to Colonel Philip Cochrane, who served with the US Air Transport Command.

Yamamoto, Isoruku

(1884–1943) Nationality: Japanese.
Senior position: Commander-in-Chief Combined Fleet.
Final rank: Admiral.

Yamamoto was without doubt the ablest Japanese naval commander of his age and a pioneer of carrier-based aviation. He served as his country's deputy navy minister from 1937 but his opposition to Japan joining the Axis powers and his lukewarm support for war with the United States made him enemies among his more expansionist peers. Despite this friction, Yamamoto was made

Above: Yamamoto pores over maps in a somewhat staged photograph taken for propaganda purposes.

commander-in-chief of the Imperial Japanese Navy's Combined Fleet, its chief strike force, in 1939.

Knowing that Japan could not win a prolonged war with the United States, he planned for a single decisive strike against Pearl Harbor to neutralize the US Pacific Fleet. He hoped this would force the United States to sue for a negotiated piece or at least give him at best six months to conduct a campaign to create a viable defensive perimeter around Japan. The attack was no more than partially successful, largely because the US carriers were not present and the base's fuel tanks were left mostly untouched. Yamamoto became increasingly pessimistic. He gambled on inflicting another decisive blow on his opponents at Midway in 1942, but the overly complex battle saw Japan lose four carriers and its best naval aviators. Yamamoto's end came in April 1943 when his aircraft was intercepted and shot down by US fighters over the Solomons.

Below: The alleged remains of Yamamoto's transport aircraft shot down over Bougainville.

Yamashita, Tomoyuki
(1885–1946) Nationality: Japanese.
Senior position: Commander
 Twenty-fifth Army.
Final rank: Lieutenant-General.

Yamashita is widely regarded as one of the best Japanese field commanders of the war. Before the outbreak of hostilities he was made inspector general of aircraft in 1940 and was also sent to Germany and Italy with a military mission. At the outbreak of the war in the Pacific his Army, which was outnumbered by two-to-one by the British, was responsible for the brilliantly conducted occupation of Malaya and Singapore that was completed in February 1942. It was a lightning campaign that won him the sobriquet "Tiger of Malaya."

Yamashita was soon sent to command in the puppet state of Manchukuo (Manchuria) and did not return to the Pacific theater until 1944, when he was tasked with defending the Philippines. His garrison fought on Luzon with considerable skill but was too weak to entirely rebuff the US invaders, and Yamashita himself was finally compelled to surrender in September 1945. On somewhat dubious grounds, he was tried for war crimes committed against civilians by out-of-control Japanese troops in Manila, found guilty, and executed.

Right: Yamashita oversaw the brilliant and swift campaign in Malaya and Singapore, the latter being Britain's worst defeat of the war.

Zeitzler, Kurt von

(1895–1963) Nationality: German.
Senior position: Chief of the General Staff.
Final rank: General.

Zeitzler earned a reputation for efficiency while serving as chief-of-staff at the army high command between 1942 and 1944, and was also lauded by Hitler for defeating the Anglo-Canadian landings at Dieppe. He was made chief of the General Staff but his reputation suffered after Kursk, an operation he had backed. After several bouts of "diplomatic" illness that prevented him from undertaking his duties, he was dismissed in July 1944.

Above: Zeitzler's advice was rarely acted upon by Hitler, who vehemently rejected his suggestion that a breakout from Stalingrad be attempted.

Zhukov, Georgi

(1896–1974) Nationality: Russian.
Senior position: Deputy Commissar
for Defense.
Final rank: Marshal.

Zhukov was the son of peasants and was conscripted into the Imperial

Russian Army in 1915, but joined the recently formed Red Army in 1918. During the interwar years he studied military science at academies in both Germany and Russia and in 1938 was given command of the Byelorussian Military District. It was at this point that he apparently narrowly avoided falling victim to Stalin's ruthless purges of the officer class because of

Above: Zkukov (left) was without doubt the greatest general to see service with the Red Army during the war.

an administrative error. He first came to public prominence when he inflicted a sharp defeat on the Japanese in Mongolia during 1939. He enhanced his reputation further with the defense of Leningrad, when he was the Red Army's chief-of-staff, during the latter stages of the largely disastrous Russo-Finnish War the same year.

He was soon recalled to Moscow and, after participating in the unsuccessful defense of Smolensk in August 1941 shortly after the opening of the German invasion, was tasked with organizing the defenses around Leningrad. His caliber was further revealed by his decisive defense of Moscow with the Western Front group of armies the following December. Zhukov subsequently held a number of both active field commands and senior staff positions for the remainder of the war but was often viewed with suspicion by Stalin.

Further victories followed over subsequent years, first at Stalingrad where he masterminded the Soviet counterattack that opened in November 1942, and then at Kursk in July 1943, where Germany's strategic armored reserve was effectively smashed in what remains the biggest armored engagement of all time. During this phase of the war Zhukov largely remained at supreme headquarters, content to draw up the broad strategy for his field command-ers to follow, but he returned to front-line action in March 1944 to engineer the drive to the Hungarian frontier. He then organized the push on Warsaw in August, which was halted due to an alleged lack of supplies. Finally, Zhukov oversaw the huge April 1945 offensive that led to the fall of Berlin. He accepted the German surrender there on 8 May

Below: Key Allied commanders, including Montgomery, Eisenhower, Zhukov (at Ike's left), and Tedder, meet in Berlin to celebrate their victory over Nazi Germany.

Index